WARGAMING IN HISTORY

WARGAMING IN HISTORY

Romans, Goths & Huns

• • • • • • •

Simon MacDowall

 Sterling Publishing Co., Inc. New York

Library of Congress Cataloging-in-Publication Data

MacDowall, Simon.
　[Goths, Huns, and Romans]
　Romans, Goths & Huns / Simon MacDowall.
　　　p.　cm. — (Wargaming in history)
　"First published in the U.K. in 1990 by Argus Books as . . . Goths, Huns, and Romans"—T.p. verso.
　Includes bibliographical references and index.
　ISBN 0-8069-8460-0
　1. War games—Design.　2. Rome—History, Military—30 B.C.-476 A.D.　3. Goths—Warfare.　4. Huns—Warfare.　I. Title.　II. Title: Romans, Goths, and Huns.　III. Series.
U310.M23　1991
793.9'2—dc20　　　　　　　　　　　　　　　　　91–20014
　　　　　　　　　　　　　　　　　　　　　　　　　　　CIP

Published in 1991 by Sterling Publishing Company, Inc.
387 Park Avenue South, New York, N.Y. 10016

© 1990 by Argus Books

Distributed in Canada by Sterling Publishing
% Canadian Manda Group, P.O. Box 920, Station U
Toronto, Ontario, Canada M8Z 5P9

First published in the U.K. in 1990 by Argus Books
as *Wargaming in History: Goths, Huns and Romans.*
Published by arrangement with Argus Books.
This edition for sale in the United States, Canada,
and the Philippine Islands only.

Manufactured in the United States of America
All Rights Reserved

Sterling ISBN 0-8069-8460-0

CONTENTS

1 SETTING THE SCENE 7
2 WARGAMES ARMIES 21
3 WARGAMES WITH MINIATURES 41
4 PAPER AND PENCIL GAMES 63
5 COMITATUS: RULES FOR MINIATURE GAMES 73
  APPENDIX: FURTHER READING 92
  INDEX 95

1 SETTING THE SCENE

CHARACTERISTICS OF THE PERIOD

'When the traditional signal to engage was sounded on both sides, a violent battle ensued. After a short exchange of missiles the Germans rushed forward brandishing their weapons and throwing themselves upon our squadrons of horse. Our men faced them stubbornly, protecting their heads with their shields, and trying to strike fear into the foe with drawn swords or the deadly javelins that they brandished. At the very crisis of battle, when our cavalry were bravely regrouping and the infantry were stoutly protecting their flanks with a wall of serried shields, thick clouds of dust arose and the fight swayed this way and that . . . Obstinately they struggled, hand to hand and shield to shield; the welkin rang with shouts of the victors and screams of the wounded. . . Then the Alamanni, having defeated and scattered our cavalry, attacked the front line of our infantry. Volleys of javelins flew hissing through the air from both sides. A uniform cloud of dust arose and obscured the field, in which arms were hurtling against arms and bodies against bodies. Yet the hail of darts and javelins and the volleys of iron-tipped arrows did not slacken although blade was clashing on blade in hand to hand conflict, breastplates were split asunder by sword blows, and wounded men who still had some blood left rose from the ground to attempt some further exploit.'

This evocative description of the Battle of Strasbourg in 357 AD, by the contemporary Roman officer Ammianus Marcellinus, captures the flavour of warfare at the twilight of the Roman Empire better than anything a modern author could convey. This battle was perhaps the last great victory of the Romans over their German enemies. Only 21 years later, the Roman army was destroyed by the Goths and their allies at the Battle of Adrianople where Ammianus tells us: 'Amid the clashing of arms and weapons on every side, Bellona was sounding the death-knell of the Roman cause.'

All periods of history have certain attractions for wargamers. This period, as the West Roman Empire collapsed in the face of barbarian pressures and internal decline, is particularly fascinating and well suited to a great variety of wargaming scenarios. It was a period that saw the gradual decline of the classical world and the emergence of what we know as the Middle Ages. The 5th Century AD, or more specifically the hundred years from about 350 to 450 AD, was perhaps the most tumultuous period in recorded history. It was a time that saw the crossing of the frozen Rhine by various German tribes; the sack of Rome by the Goths and Vandals; the great invasion of the Huns; the emergence of powerful feuding landowners and endemic peasant revolts; and, finally, the replacement of the West Roman government by various German warrior aristocracies.

This period saw the rapid deterioration of the regular Roman army at the same time as improvements in the arms and equipment of the barbarians. The Roman army became more 'Germanic', enrolling at first German recruits and later entire tribes. Meanwhile the armies of the Germanic peoples became 'Romanized' as a result of long association with the Empire and service in her armies. Warfare of the time was not a clear struggle between civilized Romans and wild barbarians. Roman armies contained large numbers of barbarians and sometimes were even entirely barbarian. On the other hand, the armies of the barbarians who had been living within the Empire for a few generations often contained Romans, and many of the barbarians themselves were veterans of the Roman army. Warfare was characterized on all sides by strong leaders with their private followings (called *comitati* or *bucellarii*) pursuing their private interests with little or no regard for who or what was barbarian or Roman.

HISTORICAL SYNOPSIS

This book is not intended to be a history of the Barbarian Invasions but rather a guide to recapturing some of the flavour and characteristics of the times through wargaming. Readers should delve deeper into some of the books recommended at the end of this book to achieve a greater understanding of the period. The following section is a very brief overview of the major

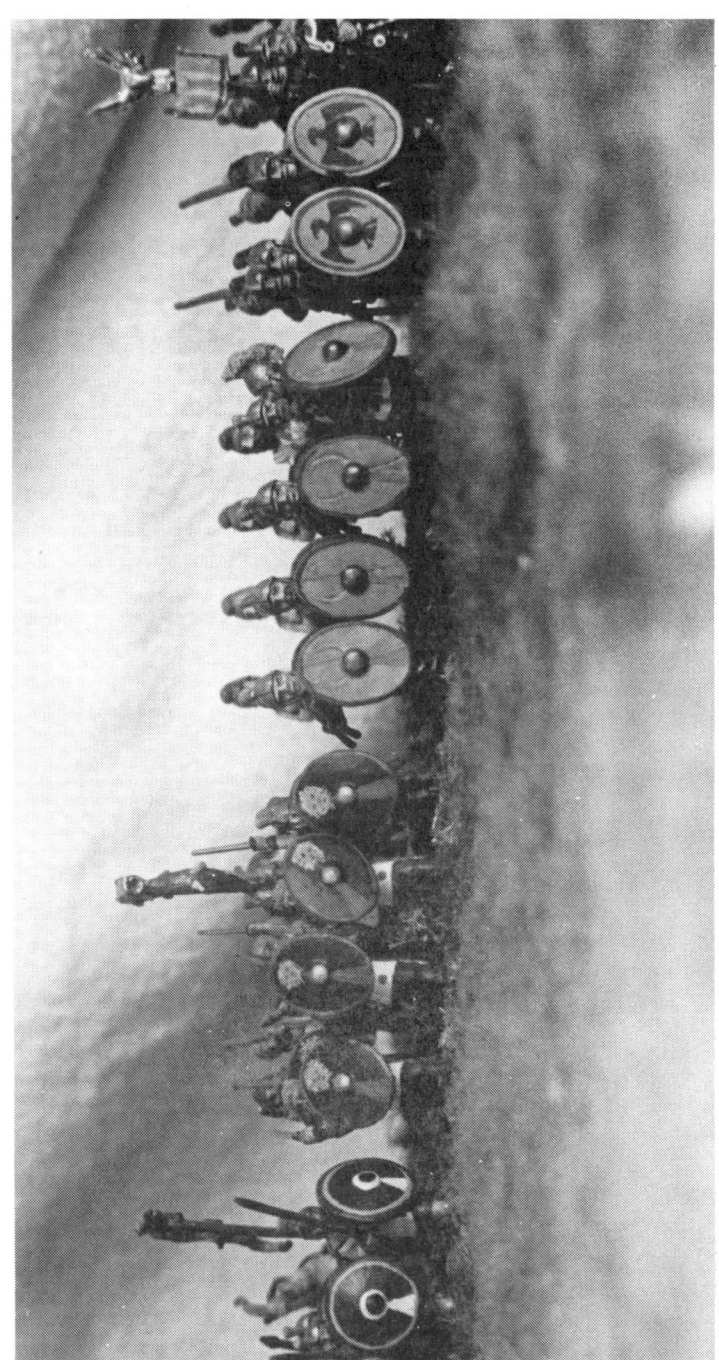

These 4th Century Palatine Infantry formed the basis of the Field Army. They include both Legions and Auxiliaries but the difference between the two was probably minimal.

events, aimed at setting the scene and providing some basic background information.

Reform of the Empire

The Emperor Augustus would not have recognized the Roman Empire of the 4th or 5th Centuries. Civil wars and economic collapse in the 3rd Century nearly destroyed the Empire. It was salvaged by the military exploits of a series of soldier-emperors from Illyria (modern Yugoslavia) and totally reformed by the Emperor Diocletian. Diocletian's reforms created an absolute monarchy, froze the economy by making all professions hereditary, and taxed the population to the limit to pay for the ever increasing demands of the army. The army, too, was reformed. The old legions and auxiliaries were given the job of defending the frontier and a new élite field army was created. This field army consisted primarily of cavalry and lighter-equipped infantry, able to respond rapidly to a crisis anywhere in the Empire.

Diocletian's reforms were carried on by his successor Constantine the Great. Constantine also moved the capital of the Empire from Rome to Byzantium, which was re-named Constantinople (present day Istanbul). But the problem of civil war had not been solved and, while Roman Generals fought each other for mastery, the German tribes on the Rhine and Danube frontiers exploited any weakness they found.

Campaigns of the 4th Century

The German tribes were growing in strength as internal strife weakened the Empire. Formerly disunited tribes were coalescing into powerful federations like the *Alamanni* (roughly meaning 'All People' in German) and their incursions became more difficult to contain. In the 350's, Julian (later Emperor) fought the Franks and Alamanni to a standstill but was forced to allow permanent settlements of Franks within the boundaries of the Empire. These Franks were settled as 'allies' under nominal Roman control. They were called *Foederati* or Federates and were to give military service in exchange for land. It was the start of what was to become a normal procedure.

In the 360's, the Emperor Julian led nearly 100,000 troops in a massive invasion of Persia that ended in disaster. Meanwhile, events on the steppes of what is now Russia ensured that the army was never given time to recover.

The Huns, a nomadic Asian people, had started to move west. They defeated the Ostrogoths, pushing them and their Visigothic cousins up against the Roman frontier. The Visigoths and some of the Vandals applied to be settled as Federates and were granted space along the Danube frontier. When the Ostrogoths asked to join them, the Romans refused, fearing a refugee problem beyond their control. Meanwhile the Visigoths, exploited by their Roman hosts, revolted and the Ostrogoths, together with some Huns and Alans, crossed the frontier to join them. This Gothic coalition destroyed the Roman army in a battle at Adrianople in 378 AD.

The Goths and the Sack of Rome

There was no effective Roman army left to stop the Goths. For several years they operated at will throughout the Balkans, their numbers swelled by Roman deserters, escaped slaves and disenchanted peasants. Eventually the Emperor Theodosius pacified them with diplomacy and allowed them to resettle as Federates within the Empire. When faced with a usurper in the West, Theodosius employed 20,000 of these Goths as the basis of his army.

On Theodosius' death in 395, the Empire was split into two halves — East and West — roughly along the line dividing the Latin and Greek-speaking parts. The following year the Visigoths, under Alaric, broke out again and ravaged Greece. After a cat and mouse type of campaign, the West Roman general Stilicho (himself the son of a Vandal) brought the Goths temporarily to bay by giving Alaric a military command and resettling his followers in northwest Greece. But this was only a temporary lull. In 402 they invaded Italy only to be beaten back by Stilicho. When Stilicho was murdered in 408 the Visigoths tried again and, in 410, they captured and sacked Rome. By this time the Emperor no longer had the strength to oppose the Visigoths, so he paid them to enter Imperial service and fight against the Vandals and Alans in Spain and France. This led to the establishment of a Visigothic Kingdom which lasted until the Arab invasion of Spain in 711 AD.

The Crossing of the Rhine and German Settlements

While Stilicho was chasing the Goths through Greece and Italy, more trouble was brewing over the frontier — the German tribes

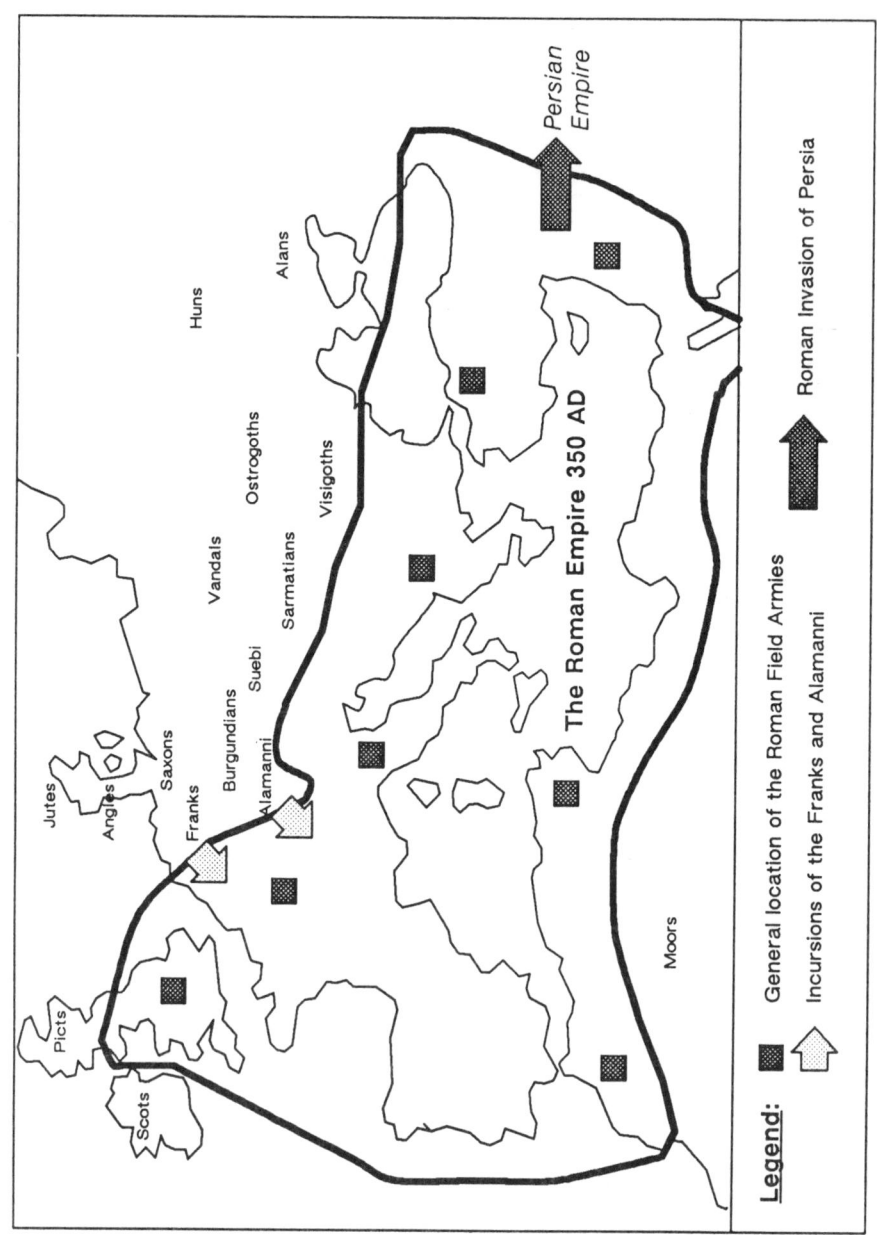

This map shows the Roman Empire at the start of the period. Pressures are already mounting on the Rhine frontier. The strength of the Roman defences are severely weakened by an abortive invasion of the Persian Empire.

were massing. The winter of 406 AD was bitterly cold and in December the Rhine froze, removing a formidable frontier obstacle. On New Year's Eve, 406, the Germans crossed the Rhine and overran the frontier. The main attack was by a coalition of Vandals and Suebi who had been joined by a clan of the Asiatic Alans. This group devastated France and continued south into Spain. But other Germans such as the Franks, Burgundians and Alamanni also crossed the collapsed frontier and seized lands for themselves on the other side of the Rhine.

There were no Roman armies strong enough to oppose the invaders. The only hope lay in the army of Britain which had revolted and proclaimed the soldier Constantine as Emperor. Constantine crossed the channel to establish himself in France, taking with him the army of Britain which was never to return. Britain was left to defend herself against the increasing attacks of the Angles, Saxons, Jutes, Picts and Scots.

By 410 the Western Empire was in a mess. The Goths were ravaging Italy and sacked Rome; the Rhine frontier had collapsed; the Vandals, Suebi and Alans had carved out kingdoms for themselves in Spain; the usurper Constantine controlled France through an alliance with the Alamanni, Franks and Burgundians; another usurper — Maximus — had set himself up in what was left of Spain; and Britain had been abandoned. The Western Emperor Honorius had made his capital at Ravenna, in northeastern Italy, where natural marshes and strong fortifications kept him safe.

A degree of order was restored by playing the various factions off against each other and formally agreeing to barbarian settlements within the Empire. The German settlements along the Rhine were left alone, and to this day German is the primary language on both sides of the Rhine, following the borders of this original settlement. The Visigoths were recognized as independent within the old borders of the Empire and were given land to settle in southwest France in return for keeping the Vandals, Suebi and Alans in check. Another clan of the Alans was settled close to the Visigothic Kingdom to act as a counterbalance to the Goths and to keep control of an increasingly rebellious population. The Celtic British (Welsh) were told to defend themselves, which they did fairly effectively for a few years under leaders such as the near-legendary Arthur, but German mercenaries called in to help defeat the Scots rebelled and established settlements in the southeast. Many of the British fled to Armorica

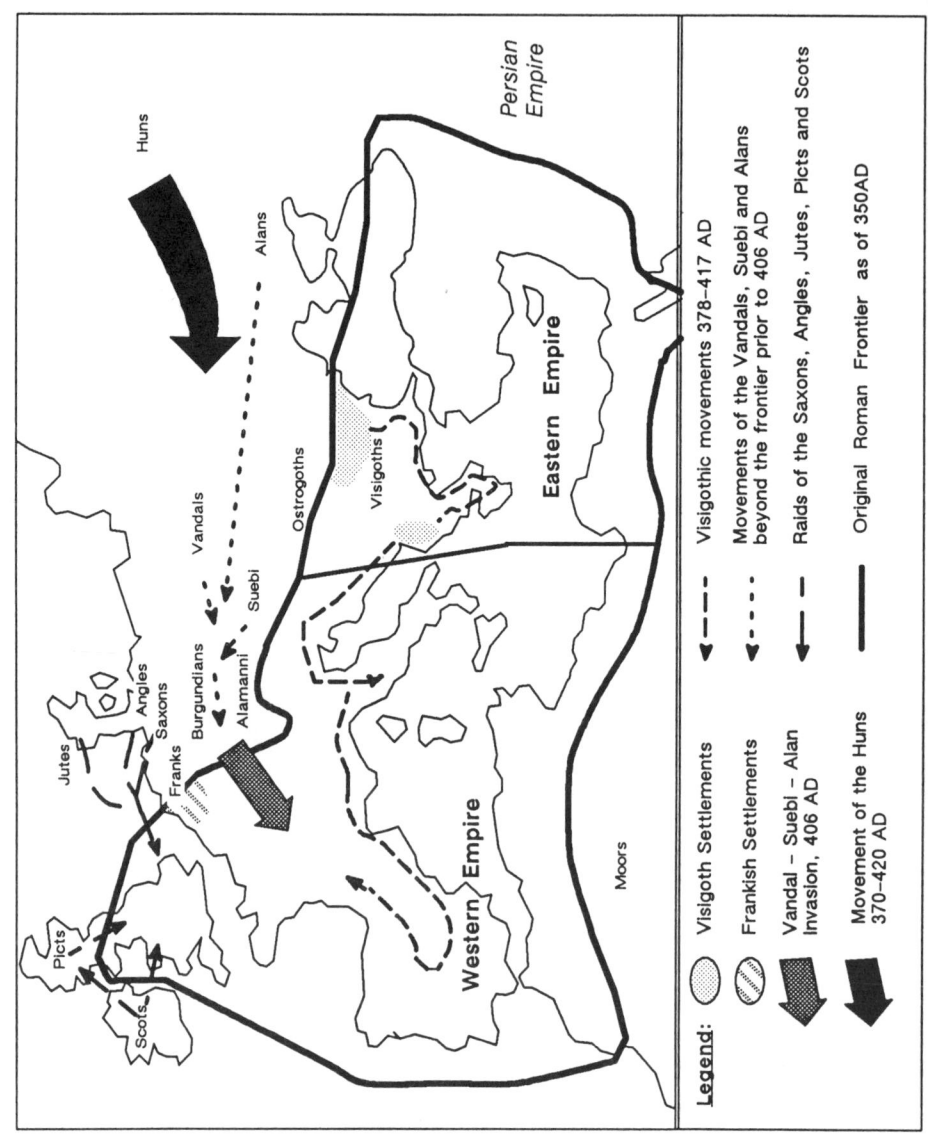

14 This map shows the Visigothic Invasion and some of the major barbarian movements up to about 410 AD

in France where they set up an independent kingdom known today as Brittany.

The Vandals remained in Spain for a number of years, but in 428 crossed into Africa where they established themselves in the fertile lands around modern Tunisia. From there, and with the help of a fleet, they were able to control the Western Mediterranean.

The Scourge of God

The Huns inspired fear in Romans and Germans alike. They were an Asiatic people, perhaps Mongolian, and their nomadic way of life was completely alien to more settled peoples. They appeared half-human in the eyes of their enemies and, unlike the previous German invaders of the Empire, they had no respect for Mediterranean civilization. The Germans, particularly the Visigoths, were looking to be accommodated within the Empire as legitimate inhabitants; the Huns destroyed what they encountered. The majority of Germans by this time were Christians and shared many of the values of Roman society, while the Huns had nothing in common with it. They were known by contemporaries as the 'Scourge of God'.

The Huns were content for a number of years to rule over a vast Empire beyond the Roman frontier, subjecting many of the German tribes, including the Ostrogoths. They often served as mercenaries in the Roman army, particularly under General Aetius who used them extensively to control the Gothic, Frankish and Burgundian settlements in France. Under the leadership of Attila, however, they started to act more aggressively. At first they raided the Eastern Empire, extracting enormous sums in 'protection money'. In 451 they turned their attention on the West. Attila led a large army of Huns and subject Germans into France. They were stopped in the Plains of Champagne, at the Battle of Chalons, by Aetius who had managed to put together an army of Romans, Franks, Visigoths, Alans, Bretons and Burgundians. The following year Attila invaded Italy but was forced to turn back by famine and the operation of an East Roman Army in his rear. Shortly after this, the great Hun died and his empire was destroyed by a revolt of his German subjects.

The End

It is probably safe to say that the Roman Empire in the West did not fall, rather it gradually faded away to be replaced by a

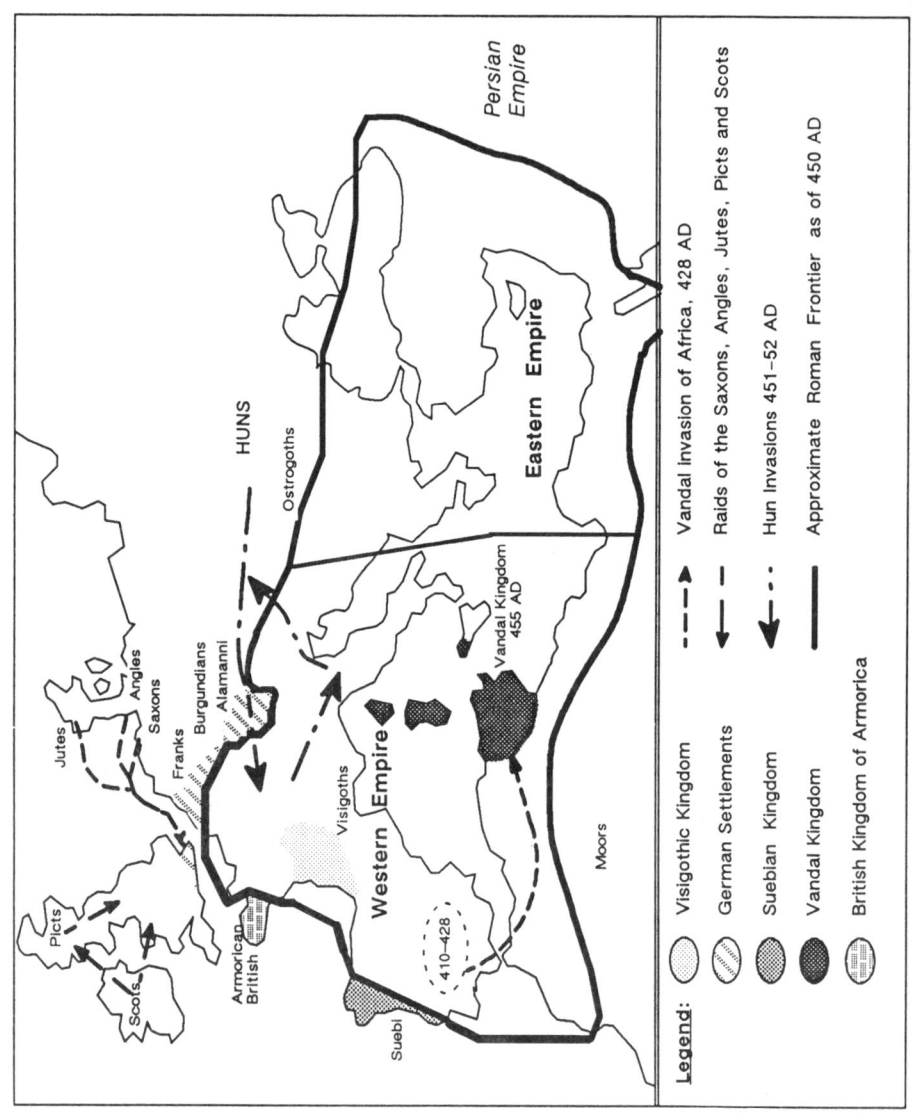

This map shows the general situation at about 455 AD. The Franks, Burgundians and Alamanni have settled both sides of the Rhine. The British who fled their homeland have established an independent kingdom in France, as have the Suebi (Swabians) in Portugal. The Vandals have moved from Spain to Africa from where they control the Mediterranean. The Visigothic Kingdom is now firmly established in southwest France and will soon expand into Spain.

number of Germanic Kingdoms, most of which continued to observe Roman customs and laws.

The Roman Army had long since ceased to be 'Roman'. Since the early 5th Century, Roman Generals relied primarily on barbarian recruits and federates to man their armies. Barbarian Generals held supreme command in these armies and the later Western Emperors were little more than puppets. In 476 AD the Roman Army in Italy deposed the Emperor Romulus Augustulus and saw no reason to replace him. Their general, Odoacer, ruled Italy independently and, although the Roman Senate continued to function for many more years, the Roman Empire in the West no longer existed. Britain had been abandoned long ago; France was fought over by the Visigoths, Franks and Gallo-Romans; Spain was in a similar situation; and Africa had been lost to the Vandals.

Odoacer's grip on Italy did not last long for, in 493, at the urging of the Eastern Emperor, the Ostrogoths moved in and established a Kingdom there which was to last up until the reconquest of Italy by the East Roman forces under Belisarius. It is worth noting here that the Eastern Empire survived this cataclysmic period intact and survived through to the capture of Constantinople by the Turks in 1453.

Magnates and Rebels

Before leaving our historical overview it is worth looking at some of the internal struggles going on inside the Empire. Perhaps one of the most fascinating aspects of the period is the growth of private armies hired by powerful landlords to protect their interests in these lawless times. Although various Emperors passed laws forbidding this, it is clear that the practice continued until it was 'legalized' in the feudal system that emerged from the wreck of Western Europe.

The social system in the Empire, introduced by Diocletian's reforms, bonded men to hereditary professions. Crushing taxes to pay for the Army brought many small farmers to ruin, and as a result they sought out the protection of these powerful landowners. In this way the farmer remained on his land, as was required by law, but the landlord took care of the tax collector and protected him from bandits, in return for him becoming a bonded serf. The only other escape from ruin was for the poor to abandon their land and become brigands. This they did in large numbers, particularly in Britain, France and Spain. These brigands were called *Bacaudae*. They became so powerful at times that they were able to sack cities, set up independent countries and mint coins. Throughout the 5th Century, particularly in France, Roman armies spent as much time trying to defeat the *Bacaudae* as defend the frontiers. In fact it is highly likely that the settlements of various barbarians, such as the Visigoths, in the heart of France far from the frontier, was for no other reason than to keep down the *Bacaudae*.

WARGAMING POSSIBILITIES

There are three common methods of wargaming, each of which can be used to recreate some of the events of this turbulent period. These methods are:

Boardgames. These are pre-packaged commercial games which consist of a game board (usually a map), rules and usually playing counters representing military units. There are a few boardgames available on the market that deal with this period, but not many. Boardgames are most useful for strategic level games covering an entire campaign. Some even span centuries in an attempt to trace the gradual decline and fall of the Roman Empire. Since boardgames are self-explanatory packages that do not require the same kind of detailed explanation as other forms of wargaming, this book will not deal with them except to make readers aware of their potential.

Paper and Pencil Games. These are games played by any number of players together with an umpire or *gamemaster*. They may take many forms and are usually run as role-playing games where players assume the role of a character from the period and interact with other players to achieve victory conditions set by the gamemaster. Popular paper and pencil games include *Committee Games* and *Postal Campaigns*. Committee games involve a group of players representing something like a council of war, trying to arrive at a decision or a series of decisions based on a scenario set by the gamemaster. They can be very simple, taking only a few minutes to play, or they can become quite involved, developing into some sort of mini-campaign. Postal campaigns are popular ways of linking wargamers who may live miles, or even continents apart. They involve making strategic decisions and mailing them in to the gamemaster who will determine the outcome. Sometimes these are used as a framework to link

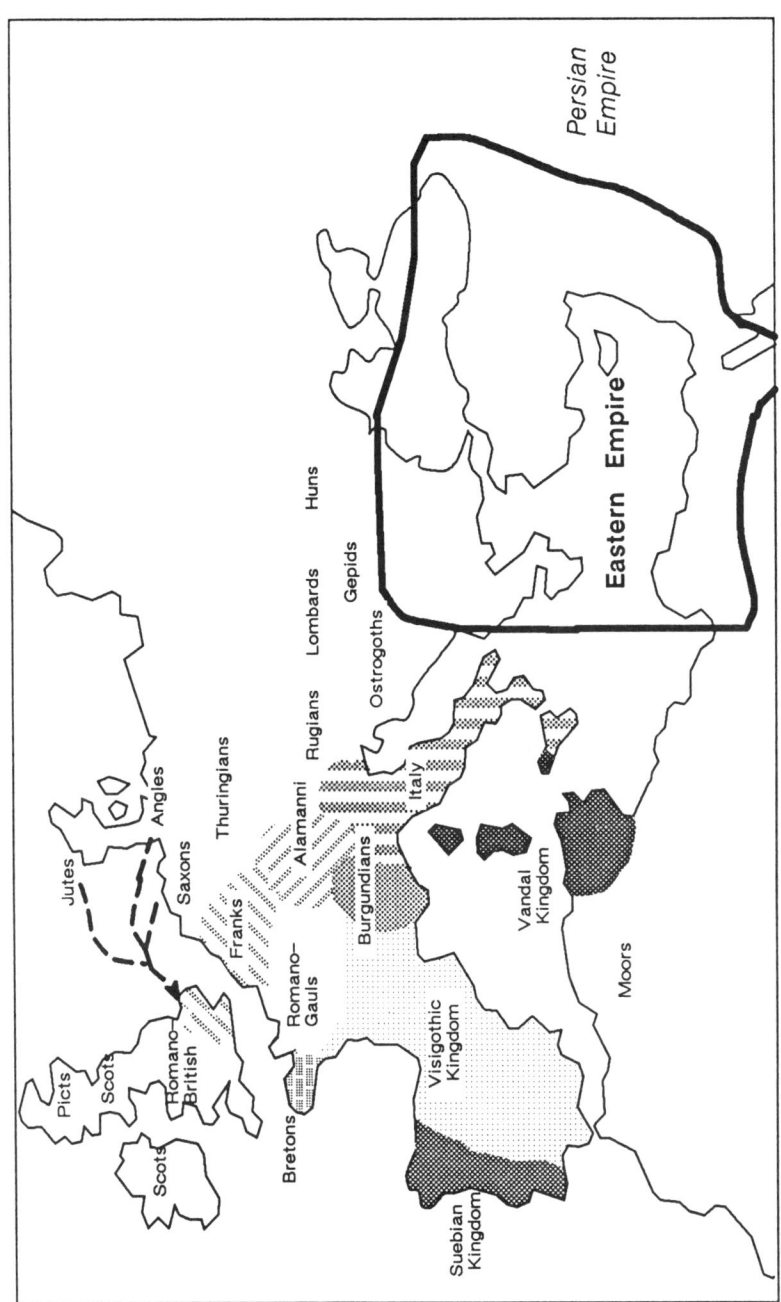

The Germanic Successor Kingdoms after the break-up of the Empire in the West in 476 AD

tactical games played with miniatures. Both of these forms of games require imagination on the part of the gamemaster and a willingness on the part of the players to immerse themselves in their roles. They will be discussed in some detail later.

Miniatures Games. These are tactical games, representing a single battle or skirmish, played out using scale model figures. The games are sometimes linked together to form a campaign. Figures are available commercially in a variety of scales from 2mm to 54mm — these being the approximate height of the figures. Most wargames are fought using 15mm or 25mm figures with 6mm becoming popular for large battles. Rules are available commercially which provide methods of fighting battles with miniatures for the *Ancient Period* but specific rules for this particular period are rare. I have produced one set called *Comitatus,* which deals specifically with the Barbarian Invasions. It is included in its entirety as Chapter 5. Wargaming with miniatures is perhaps the most involved method of wargaming since it includes the collecting and painting of models as well as playing. For this reason most of the book will be devoted to miniatures games. The effort is, however, well worth it, since the colour and effect of deploying an army of well-painted figures captures a greater feel for any historical period than any of the other methods described. Such games do however have their limitations and wargamers should bear in mind that games with miniatures can only recreate fairly low-level tactical engagements. To explore all aspects of warfare of this period players should combine miniatures battles with paper and pencil games and boardgames.

2 WARGAMES ARMIES

HISTORICAL ARMIES

The Roman Army

The Roman Army at the start of this period was a well-organized force in spite of the fact that many units bore tribal names. The army had been totally reorganized by the Emperors Diocletian and Constantine and bore little resemblance to the more familiar armies of the Republic or early Empire. The key to this reorganization had been the creation of a mobile field army that could respond quickly to any threat while more static border troops manned the frontier, holding strong points until they could be relieved.

The Border troops, known as *Limitanei* (troops based along the *Limes* or frontier) and *Ripenses* (troops stationed along river frontiers), were the old Legions and Auxiliaries that had been based in static defensive positions since the days of Hadrian. They were no longer the élite mobile forces that we associate with their names, but rather closer to a part-time militia that had settled down on the land to farm and raise families while at the same time providing a local defence for the region.

The Field Army (*Palatini* who were initially the Emperor's centralized forces, and *Comitatenses* who were regional field forces) on the other hand, was a highly mobile force based in the cities and towns of the interior. It was composed primarily of Auxiliaries and Cavalry but also a few newly-created units bearing the title of 'Legions'. These Legions, however, were far removed from their predecessors, being only 1000-1500 men strong (as opposed to 5,000 under Julius Caesar) and having a greater reliance on long range missile weapons.

It was this army that Julian led to victory against the Alamanni at the Battle of Strasbourg at the start of our period, and which was destroyed at the Battle of Adrianople by the Goths in 378 AD.

Legionary Forts along the frontier became permanent bases manned by a part time militia (Limitanei) who farmed the frontier districts and provided a local defence force that could hold on to strong points providing a firm base for the more mobile Field Army.

The Gravestone of Lepontius, a Fourth Century Roman Soldier from Strasbourg. He carries a short spear with a very broad blade. He is unarmoured with a long-sleeved tunic and cloak and carries a fairly large round shield. His helmet is curious. It appears to have two round holes near the top and a single feather as a plume. It is difficult to say what it would have looked like. The cockerel in the background seems to be a standard. This figure is perhaps representative of the *Limitanei* of the Rhine frontier. (*Musée Archéologique, Strasbourg*)

The army never recovered from the disaster at Adrianople although it survived on paper for a few more decades. From the 5th Century on, Roman commanders were forced to rely on ever increasing numbers of barbarian federates as the backbone of their followings. Roman troops were still in existence, but it is clear from the writings of contemporary authors such as Vegitius and Procopius that they were of little value, demoralized by defeat and poorly trained.

The German Armies

The Germans had a number of common characteristics, with some specific differences between tribes. The core of all German armies was the *comitatus* of the kings and nobles. These were the sworn companions of a leader, full-time warriors who would have been well armed and equipped. With the notable exception of the Saxons in Britain, the *comitati* would normally have been cavalry. The majority of other warriors would have been part-time soldiers, probably without armour. These followers could have fought either on foot or horseback. The Ostrogoths, Vandals, Gepids and Lombards were noted for having a greater reliance on cavalry than the other Germans.

Those nations which had settled for a long time within the Empire, such as the Visigoths after the establishment of their kingdom in 417, would have borne little resemblance to the tribes that had crossed the Rhine or Danube generations before. Tribal organization was replaced by a more ordered society governed by laws written by Roman civil servants and headed by a king. Their armies attracted peoples of other races including Roman deserters and runaway serfs. Gallo-Romans are mentioned fighting in 5th Century Visigothic armies, and the Roman author Procopius tells about formed Roman units in Frankish armies of the 6th Century, still identifiable by their standards and shield designs.

The Vandals, who eventually settled in Africa, were entirely a shock cavalry force. Procopius notes that they were unable to respond to skirmishers, having no missile-armed troops of their own. They did, however, employ lightly-armed Moorish auxiliaries on occasion. Other German nations certainly did use missile troops. The Alamanni, Goths and Lombards employed fairly large numbers of foot archers, usually from the poorer classes of their society.

The Alamanni were noted by Ammianus as retaining the tactic

Infantry was the mainstay of most German armies, particularly those in the West. Here a Saxon King is surrounded by his sworn companions (*Comitatus*). Troops of lesser social standing fill in the rear ranks of the formation.

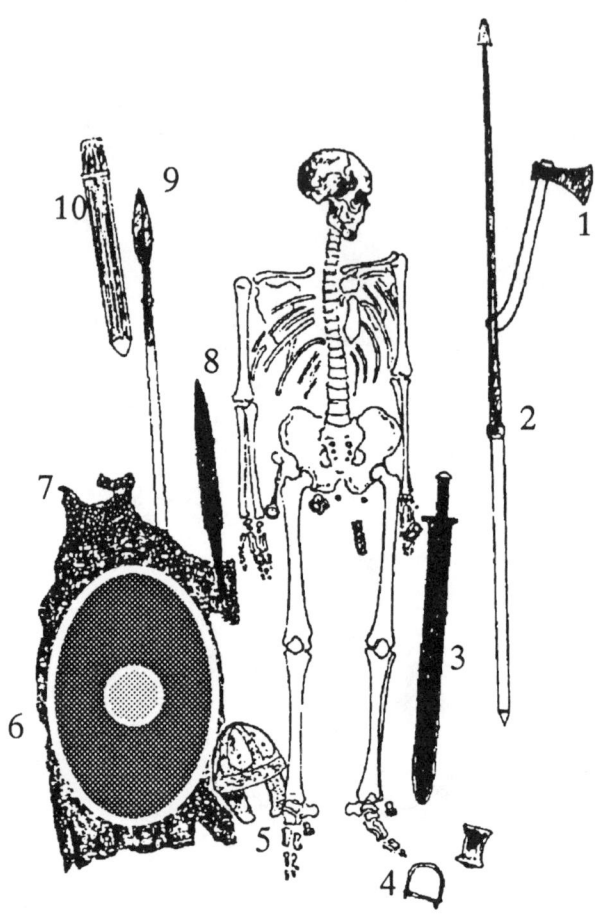

Grave Goods of an Alamannic Noble
1. Francisca
2. Angon
3. Spatha
4. Horse Furniture
5. Helmet
6. Shield
7. Chain mail shirt
8. Sax
9. Spear
10. Arrows

German archeologists have classified the grave goods of the Alamanni warriors into three classes:
1. The poor, who would be buried only with bow and arrows;
2. The majority who would have a spear, shield and sax (short sword); and
3. The rich who would add spatha (broad sword) angon (heavy javelin) or francisca (throwing axe) and perhaps armour and horse furniture.
—From *Die Alamannen* by Rainer Christlein.

of the earlier Germans of mixing fit young foot warriors with their cavalry to increase their effectiveness in combat. Some other Germans may have done the same thing.

The Asiatics

The Huns at their height ruled over a vast empire. Their subjects included Slavs, Ostrogoths, Gepids, Thuringians and many other German and Asiatic peoples. All of these nations fought in the Hunnic army in their own style, the Huns themselves being nomadic mounted archers.

The Alans seem to have fought as typical steppe horse archer skirmishers, in a similar manner to the Huns. Various clans of the Alans were at times allied with the Vandals, Goths, Huns and Romans.

It is quite possible that, while the majority of the Huns and Alans were light horse archers, some nobles may have fought as shock cavalry. There is even mention of horse armour among the Alans.

SELECTING YOUR ARMY

So which army is the right one for you to wargame with? Obviously if you have some historical sympathies you should wargame with the army that you can identify with. You may, for example, identify with someone like Stilicho or even Arthur, fighting a losing battle as the remnants of civilization fade under barbarian pressure; or perhaps you favour the free Germanic warriors fighting against a corrupt and bureaucratic society. These are, of course, stereotypes but the point is that you should wargame with an army with which you can sympathize.

If you have no such sympathies you should look at how the army suits your personality. A German army, for example, is very straightforward. You cannot accomplish many fancy manoeuvres with it as the vast majority of the troops are most useful in a frontal charge. Your best tactic is to line up your troops, charge home as soon as possible and smash the opposition. An Asiatic army, on the other hand, is quite the opposite. With hordes of light horse archers you have very few troops who can charge blindly forward sweeping the enemy from the field. Rather, you will have to wear down your opponent in a drawn-out skirmishing action until he is sufficiently weakened that your troops can charge home. A Roman army is much more balanced, containing a mix of shock and skirmish troops allowing you to conduct

While most Asiatic troops were highly mobile cavalry archers, some of the more wealthy nobles, like those shown here, would have been armoured shock cavalry.

sneaky manoeuvres or stand up to hand-to-hand combat.
Most wargamers seem to favour the Roman army of the 4th Century where the troops are still reliable and there is a reasonable balance of troop types. This is unfortunate because the more colourful barbarian and 5th Century armies tend to get overlooked. I personally like tricky manoeuvres and my favourite army is the Army of Aetius in France — a combination of Huns, Alans, Franks and Goths and hardly a real Roman among them! For beginners, though, I would recommend a German infantry based army — such as the Franks or Alamanni — because it is very easy to operate on the wargames table as well as being quite easy to paint.

Figures

Selecting figures in any scale for this period is an easy task because differences between warriors were few. Barbarians were often raiding parties of mixed nationality who had equipped themselves from Roman factories and the battlefield. Fashions were copied: all wore the popular *spangenhelm* helmet with nose and cheek guards; longsleeved tunics and long trousers were an almost universal dress; the *spatha,* the favourite sword of Roman and German alike; shield bosses, belt buckles and brooches of similar pattern were worn by warriors of any nationality; Roman leaders gave gifts of clothing to their followers — including barbarian federates. So the wargamer in this period should not limit himself to what the figure manufacturers call their products. A barbarian warband should show a sprinkling of Roman equipment, clothing and shield designs. Roman armies should include auxiliaries looking very similar to Germans or Huns but perhaps with a few pieces of uniform equipment, such as shields. The *Comitati* of Roman commanders would probably be Germans or, in the case of Aetius, Huns. A German *Comitatus,* on the other hand, would most likely be completely decked out in captured or copied Roman armour. The armies of the Barbarian Invasions are a figure converter's dream!

UNIFORMS AND EQUIPMENT

There are a number of publications available which provide information on the dress and equipment of this period. The most useful is *Armies and Enemies of Imperial Rome* by Phil Barker. This publication covers all the major combatants of the Bar-

A line of 5th Century Roman Infantry. By this time the infantry played a subordinate role to cavalry on the battlefield. Their job was to hold ground and perhaps provide missile support while the cavalry delivered the decisive blow. They were no longer employed offensively as in the old days of the Legions.

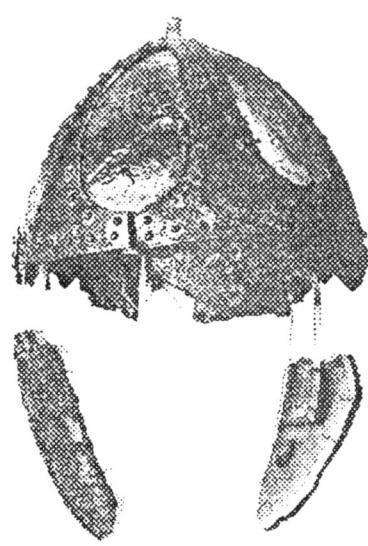

A *spangenhelm* helmet found near Strasbourg, site of Julian's battle with the Alamanni. (*Musée Archéologique, Strasbourg*)

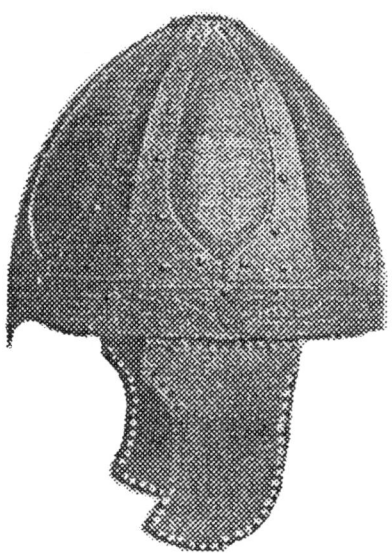

A similar *spangenhelm* from Northern Italy showing how widespread the style was. (*Museo di Bargello, Florence*)

barian Invasions period and includes a large selection of shield designs. Barker also presents a logical argument for Roman uniform colours, which I will not repeat here, but suffice it to say that he concludes that Roman auxiliaries and cavalry had off-white tunics, brown trousers, and yellow crests on their helmets (when worn), Legionaries had red tunics and red crests. Cloaks, when worn, were yellow-brown.

Much less is known about barbarian clothing colours. Natural linens and wools were probably the norm amongst the rank and file while the nobility seem to have gone in for bright colours.

There is some debate as to how much armour was worn. Ammianus Marcellinus, in describing the 4th Century Roman and Alamannic armies, often talks about breast plates and glittering armour — how much of this is poetic and how much is descriptive we don't know. In his descriptions of the 5th Century Roman army, Vegitius says that the Roman infantry had abandoned all armour, even helmets. Monuments and tombstones tend to confirm Vegitius while showing that many cavalrymen were armoured. My own reconstruction of the available evidence is that in the 4th Century Roman army up to Adrianople, at least some infantrymen wore armour. This was possibly more common in the Legions than the Auxiliaries. This armour could have been either mail or rawhide — the familiar segmented armour having dropped out of use in the 3rd Century. Cavalry were more heavily armoured, scale or mail armour being common, although fairly large numbers of light skirmish cavalry were also used.

Armour was probably fairly common among the members of a war leader's *Comitatus,* whether German, Hun or Roman. Chainmail shirts and helmets have been found in the graves of German nobles but most grave finds include only a spear and shield. From this we may conclude perhaps that the rank and file of a barbarian unit were unarmoured.

Catafractarii and Clibanarii

Some Roman cavalry were very heavily armoured and rode armoured horses. These troops, called cataphracts, have been the subject of some controversy. It appears as though there were several types of cataphracts and you cannot get two historians to agree on what exactly they were. Without going deeply into the various arguments, my own opinion follows.

There were two main types of cataphracts: *Equites Catafractarii* and *Equites Clibanarii*. The *Equites Catafractarii* have Gallic

A Roman Cavalry wing is deployed for battle. Light cavalry are on the right flank and the General remains in reserve with his bodyguard and some heavily armoured Clibanarii.

A Selection of Roman Soldiers 350-450 AD

Cavalryman 4th-5th C AD
Equites Armigeri

Infantryman 5th C AD
Auxilia Celtae

Infantryman 4th C AD
Auxilia Brisigari

These figures show representative Roman Soldiers from the Barbarian Invasions period. They no longer resemble the more familiar Legionaries of earlier times. The Cavalry are the most heavily armoured. Infantry gradually gave up wearing armour, first abandoning body defences and later even helmets. The cavalryman wears a version of what is known as the Spangenhelm helmet, it was also very popular with both German and Asiatic barbarians. The circular patches on the tunic hems, and shoulder patches partially visible on the 4th C infantryman, are standard decorations worn by many soldiers and civilians at the time. The Shield designs and unit names are known to us from a document called the Notitia Dignitatum. This was written in the 5th C and lists all the field army units along with their shield patterns. The Germanic appearance of these soldiers is quite pronounced, most of them could just as easily be in a German army.

names (such as the *Equites Catafractarii Biturigenses*) and all appear to have originated from Gaul (France) although they later primarily saw service in the east. *Catafractarii* units first appeared under the Emperor Hadrian in the 2nd Century and it is highly likely that they were Sarmatian federates who had been settled in France. Later *Catafractarii* were probably their descendants and additional units modelled on them. If this was the case then these troops were probably heavily armoured lancer cavalry like the Sarmatians, but not necessarily riding armoured horses.

Clibanarii appeared much later and it would seem that there were two types. Some, such as the *Equites Sagittarii Clibanarii* and the *Equites Persae Clibanarii,* were probably modelled on the Persian heavy cavalry of the same name and were armed with bows. They may have had armoured horses but it is equally possible that they did not. Other *Clibanarii*, from the descriptions of Ammianus, were clearly completely armoured lancers riding armoured horses. These were probably modelled on the Palmyran or Parthian Cataphracts such as the *Cuneus Equitum Clibanariorum Palmirenorum.*

SAMPLE ARMIES

Researching and building an army can be one of the most enjoyable aspects of the hobby, on the other hand it is often difficult for the beginner to know where to start. The following section is intended to give examples of *starting points* for typical armies of the period. I have given unit sizes in number of stands, assuming a double rank infantry stand described on pages 36-37.

Scale A useful scale for larger battles is one infantry stand (8 figures) representing roughly 500 men, and cavalry or light infantry stands (2-4 figures) representing 250-300 men. This allows an Auxiliary Cohort (500 men) to be represented by one stand, a Legion (1000-1500 men) by two to three stands and a Cavalry *Vexillation* (600 men) by two stands. We do not know the size of barbarian units, if indeed 'units' were used. I tend to make them larger than their Roman counterparts since all indications point to fairly large inflexible organizations. Two to four stands works well.

4th Century Roman Field Army
Typical field armies in the West seem to have contained about three times as many infantry as cavalry units. Among the

SUGGESTED BASING FOR FIGURES

Most wargamers base their figures on multiple stands and use these as the basis of their wargames units. For Ancient wargaming a standard base of 6cm frontage and variable depth has been adopted. I like to mount infantry in two ranks and cavalry in a single rank as shown in the diagrams below. These diagrams are drawn to actual size for 25mm figures: either 6cm x 4cm or 6cm x 6cm. Bases for 15mm and 6mm figures would be 4cm x 3cm and 4cm x 4cm. 15mm bases would use the same figure arrangements as shown below while the number of figures per base would be doubled for 6mm figures.

Combat Infantry Stand
Eight figures in two ranks are mounted on the base. This would be appropriate for a Roman Infantry unit arranged in fairly regular ranks and files.

Combat Cavalry Stand
Here three cavalry figures are mounted on a base. This could represent cavalry of any army.

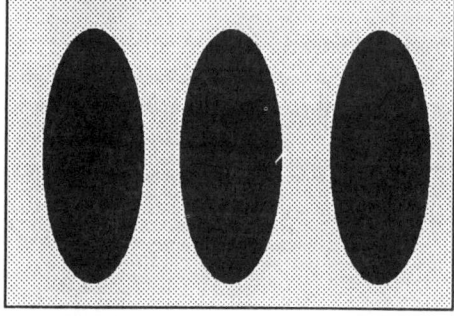

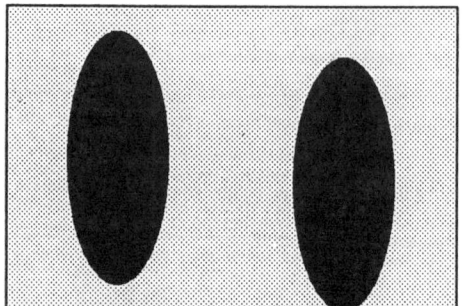

Light Cavalry Stand
Light skirmishing cavalry such as Horse Archers could be more loosely based with only two figures per stand.

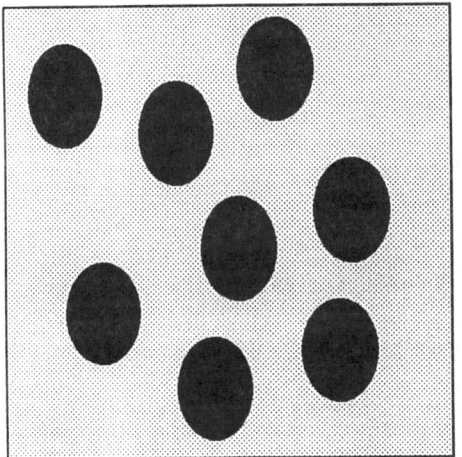

Barbarian Infantry Stand
This is an alternate basing arrangement that I prefer for Barbarian Infantry. The 6cm deep base allows for a looser, more irregular effect.

Alternate Cavalry Stand
Using a deeper base for cavalry also allows for a more irregular effect and can be used for barbarian cavalry or light cavalry.

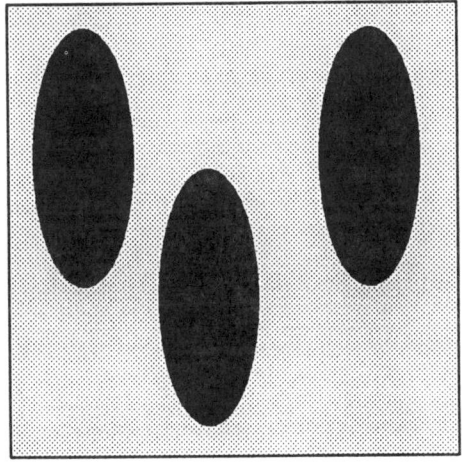

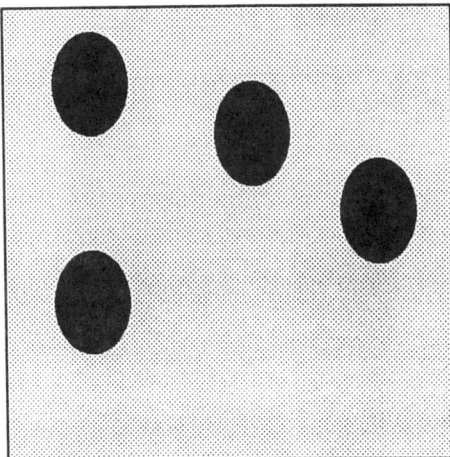

Skirmisher Stand
Four figures are mounted in two ranks. Since these represent light infantry, they should be spaced out irregularly on the base even if Romans. Alternatively the four figures could be based on a 4cm deep stand.

infantry, there were about twice as many Auxiliaries as Legions. In the East, the proportion of cavalry would have been higher and there were more horse archers and cataphracts. Border troops would probably have been fairly similar to their field army counterparts but with lower morale.

General and Comitatus One stand Roman cavalry, armed with javelins and/or spears, probably armoured although some Roman Guard cavalry were light. They would probably be fairly Germanic in appearance. High morale.

Heavy Cavalry One unit of two stands armoured Roman cavalry with javelins and/or spears. Average to high morale.

Light Cavalry One unit of two stands unarmoured Roman cavalry with javelins. Average to high morale.

Auxiliaries Two units each of one stand unarmoured Roman infantry with javelins. Poor to average morale.

Legionaries One unit of two stands armoured or unarmoured Roman infantry with javelins. Poor to average morale.

Archers One unit of two stands unarmoured Roman light infantry with bows. These could be fielded as an independent unit or attached to the infantry, firing overhead from a rear rank. Poor to average morale.

Additions To increase the size of this army you should consider more auxiliaries and conventional cavalry and perhaps a unit of javelin armed skirmishers, light horse archers or cataphracts.

Alamannic Army

The Alamanni were the main enemy of the 4th Century Romans in the West and remained a powerful force right through to the 6th Century. Other German tribes, such as the Visigoths, would have been similar.

General and Comitatus One unit of two stands armoured German cavalry with spears and javelins. Very high morale.

Cavalry One unit of two stands German cavalry with spears and/or javelins. Probably a mix of armoured and unarmoured troops. Could have light infantry javelinmen mixed in with them. High morale.

Infantry One unit of four stands German infantry. Most unarmoured spearmen but a few better armoured figures in the front ranks armed with heavy javelins (angons) or throwing axes (franciscae). You could also mix in a few archers in the rear ranks. Average to high morale.

Archers One unit of two stands German light infantry. Unarmoured archers. Poor to average morale.

Additions You should probably increase units in roughly the same proportion as above. Javelin armed skirmishers could also be added.

5th Century Roman Army

This army could contain just about anything, as commanders made use of whatever troops and mercenaries were available. You could, for example, build an army entirely of Huns and call it a Roman army at the time of Aetius! The sample that follows could be the core of an army in France under Aetius at about 430 AD.

General and Comitatus One unit of two stands Hun Cavalry armed with bows and spears, probably armoured. Very high morale.

Huns One unit of four stands light horse archers. High morale.

Roman Cavalry One unit of two stands Roman heavy or light cavalry (as per 4th Century army). Average morale.

Roman Infantry One unit of two stands unarmoured Roman infantry with spears or javelins. Poor morale.

Roman Archers One unit of two stands unarmoured Roman archers. Poor morale. Could be attached to the infantry unit.

Additions: You could add just about any troops to flush out this army. German infantry and cavalry (Franks or Alamanni) would be a good addition as would Alans (similar to the Huns). Aetius' army that stopped Attila at Chalons contained Franks, Burgundians, Armorican British, Alans and Goths.

Attila's Army

The army that Attila led into Gaul in 451 was a coalition of Huns, Ostrogoths, Gepids and other Germans.

Attila and Comitatus One unit of two stands Hun armoured cavalry with lances and bows. Very high morale.

Hun Cavalry Two units each of four stands Hun unarmoured cavalry with bows. High morale.

German Cavalry Two units each of two stands German cavalry armed with spears and/or javelins. Probably a mix of armoured and unarmoured troops. Poor to average morale.

Additions: The German contingents could be expanded into Ostrogothic and Gepid contingents each under their own commanders. German infantry, such as Thuringians and Franks, could also be included. German contingents could include archers. The number of actual Huns could also be increased. Morale of German units should be lower than normal because they were not enthusiastic allies.

3 WARGAMES WITH MINIATURES

SET PIECE TABLETOP BATTLES

Tabletop games with miniatures, where two armies of roughly equal strength meet in a set piece battle, are probably the most common form of wargame. Such battles can be made more interesting by linking them together in a campaign or by developing a scenario in which a degree of historical realism is injected. Actually, large set piece battles were rare in this period, particularly after the 4th Century. There were, however, some battles that could be adapted to wargaming.

The Battle of Strasbourg, 357 AD (Argentoratum)

This battle was described in the opening paragraph of this book. The West Roman army in France, about 13,000 strong, marched to stop the Alamanni who had crossed the Rhine near Strasbourg. The Alamanni were reported to be 35,000 strong and probably included other German allies such as the neighbouring Suebi (Swabians).

The Battle as a Wargame. This is a very good introductory battle. It was a fairly straightforward affair between two balanced armies with equal chances of victory. As infantry was the basis of both forces, manoeuvre is quite simple and can easily be reproduced by beginners to the period. Our information of the forces involved is also relatively complete, thanks to the account of Ammianus.

We know, for example, that the Roman army contained at least a *Clibanarii* unit, the *Primani* Legion and four Auxiliary units: *Cornuti, Bracchiati, Batavi* and *Regii*. From descriptions of campaigns prior to the battle we can also be fairly certain that two cavalry units, the *Gentiles* and *Scutarii*, and several additional auxiliary units — *Petulantes, Celtae* and *Heruli* — were

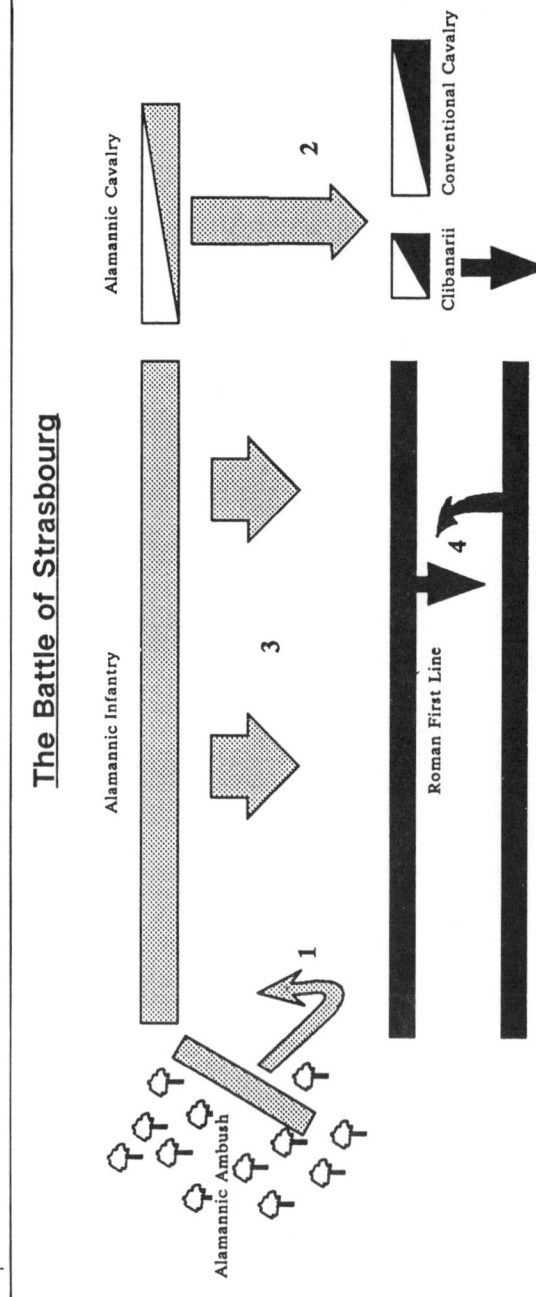

also present. We also know the names of the key commanders: Chnodommar was the Alamannic commander-in-chief and commanded the left flank cavalry, and his nephew Serapio commanded the right wing ambush. There were another five Alammanic kings present in the battle who presumably commanded their own contingents in the centre. They were: Vestralp, Urius, Ursicinus, Suomar and Hortar. On the Roman side, Severus commanded the left wing and Julian was commander-in-chief, probably on the right. Also present was Florentinius the praetorian prefect.

The Battle of Adrianople, 378 AD (Hadrianopolis)

The East Roman Emperor, Valens, moved to deal with a combined army of Visigoths, Ostrogoths, Alans and perhaps a few Huns. Rather than wait for reinforcements from the West, Valens decided to attack immediately and gain credit for victory himself. The battle took place on 9 August 378 on a very hot day in what is now the European part of Turkey (ancient Hadrianopolis is the modern city of Erdine).

The Roman Army in column of march encountered the barbarian camp which consisted of a laager of wagons formed in a protective circle, like the wagon trains of the American west. Fritigern, the Gothic commander, was defending the laager with Visigothic infantry. The cavalry of the Ostrogoths and Alans were out foraging. As the Romans advanced, he sent messengers to call the cavalry back, and started negotiation with the Romans to gain time.

The cavalry of the Ostrogoths and Alans, commanded by Alatheus and Saphrax, were out foraging. As the Romans approached, Fritigern tried to stall for time through negotiations but the Roman advance guard, consisting of archers and light cavalry commanded by Cassio and Bacurius, attacked from the line of march. Eventually the Gothic cavalry returned and hit the Romans in the flank. It was the worst Roman defeat since Cannae.

The Battle as a Wargame. One problem with re-fighting a historical battle is that, if players know what happened historically, they have the benefit of hindsight not available to the actual generals. This is a particular problem with this battle because, if the Roman commander knows that the enemy cavalry is off foraging,

The Battle of Adrianople

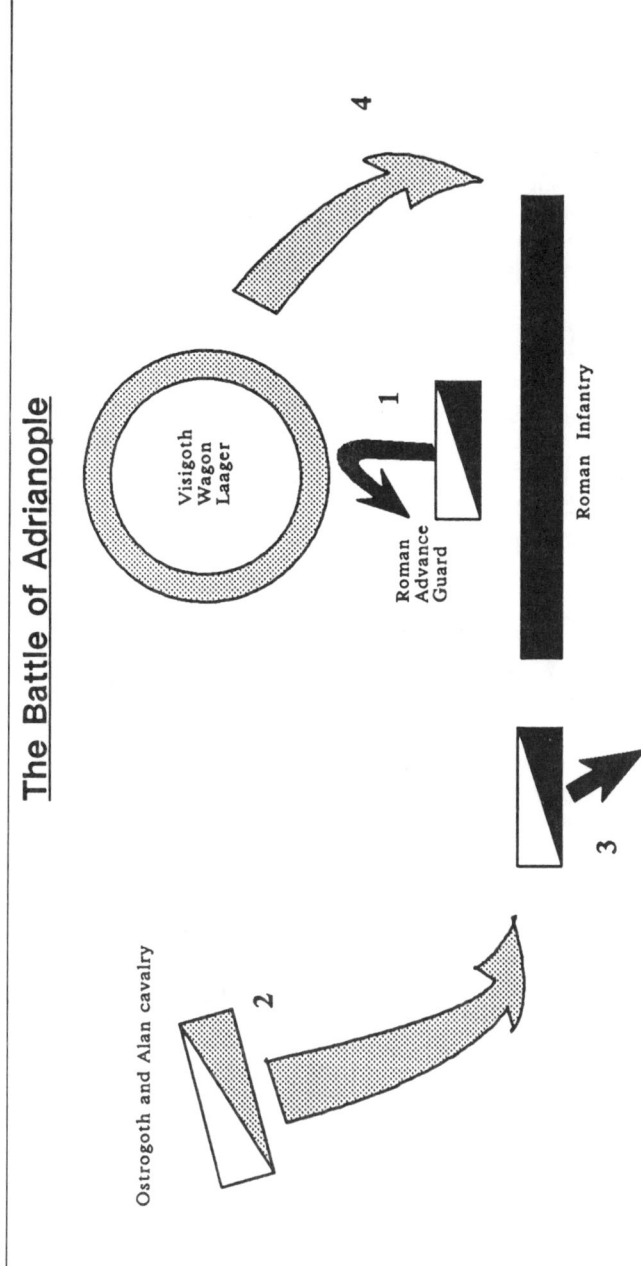

1. The Roman advance guard attacks immediately without waiting for the main body to form up. They are repulsed from the wagon laager by the Visigoths who are defending it.
2. The Ostrogoth and Alan cavalry return as the Roman advance guard is being driven back.
3. The Roman cavalry on the flanks are driven off.
4. The Roman Infantry is encircled and destroyed. The Emperor Valens is killed.

he will take precautions that he would not normally have taken. One way of getting around this is to disguise the scenario, pretending it is something else. In this way, players who know their history can still be surprised.

The Battle of Adrianople can quite easily be disguised as the Battle of Strasbourg. The Gothic commander will be told he is fighting Adrianople but the Roman commander will be told he is fighting Strasbourg. In the briefing to the Roman commander he will be told that he is approaching the 'barbarian' position in column of march. There should be woods on the flank in order to lead him to suspect an ambush there. The Gothic cavalry will, however, be off the table on the opposite flank. The Visigoth infantry should be formed up in a strong defensive position, perhaps uphill, but without a wagon laager as that would give the game away. What the Roman player sees then, is an infantry army in a position that resembles Strasbourg. He will be inclined to attack without suspecting cavalry reinforcements, exactly as Valens did. The Goth will, of course, know that it is the battle of Adrianople but he should not reveal this to his opponent.

The troops involved in this battle offer an interesting mix on the barbarian side. There are Visigothic infantry, Ostrogothic heavy cavalry and Alan horse archers. It is probably one of the best balanced non-Roman armies of the period.

The Battle of Chalons (Campus Mauriacus)

After years of raiding the Eastern Empire and extracting tribute, the Huns, led by Attila, attacked the West. Attila gathered together a huge army including various German vassal states, notably the Ostrogoths, Gepids, Ripuarian Franks and Thuringians. The West Romans had few resources left to oppose him as Aetius, virtual ruler of the West, had relied on Hunnic mercenaries to form the core of his armies. Aetius managed to form an alliance with his former enemies the Visigoths, and together with the other peoples of France (Alans, Salian Franks, Burgundians and Armorican Britons) marched to stop the Huns who crossed the Rhine in 451.

The Huns advanced on Orleans where they hoped the Alans would join them but Aetius got there first and enlisted the Alans on his side. Attila then fell back to the plains of Champagne where he could find open terrain that would favour his cavalry army. A number of skirmishes occurred along the way, most notably between the Franks of Aetius and Gepids of Attila, in

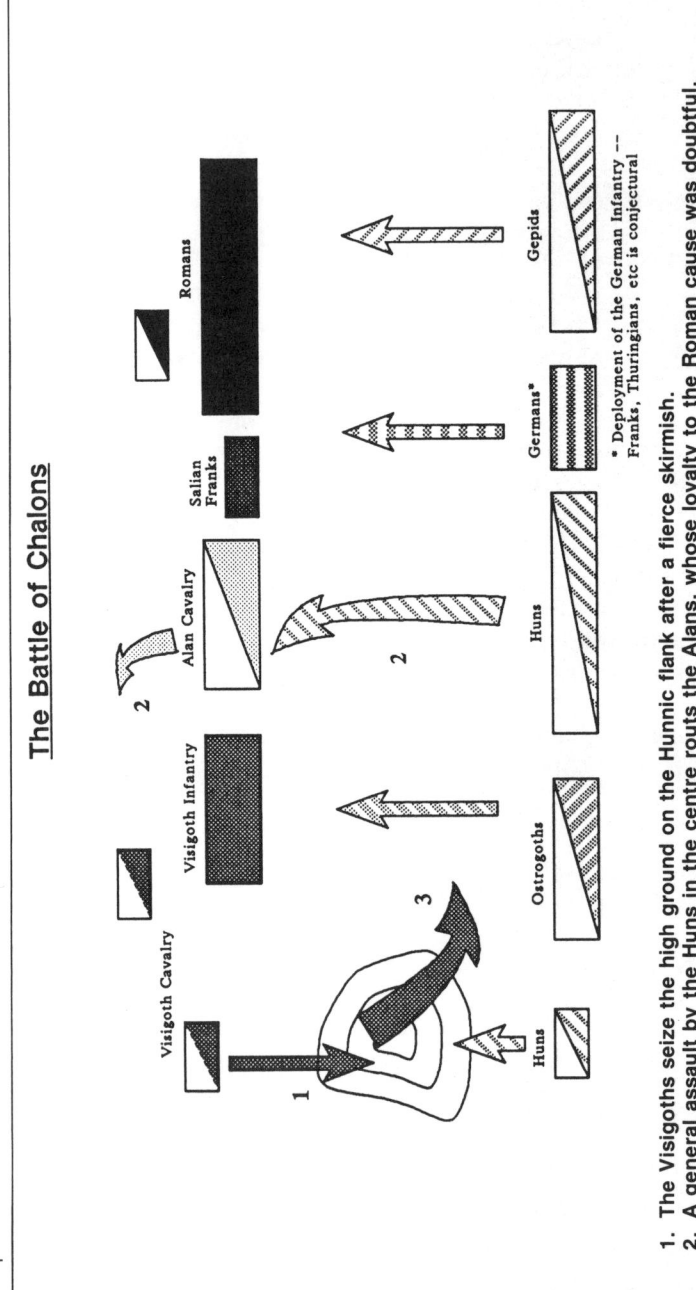

which 15,000 men are reported to have been killed.
Battle was joined at the Campus Mauriacus in Champagne, possibly near modern day Chalons. Attila was defeated after a long, hard battle but the Western allies were too exhausted to pursue.

The Battle as a Wargame. This is an excellent multi-player game as the various commanders involved are independent allies. They include, on the Roman side:
Aetius, commander-in-chief and commander of the Romans and smaller allied contingents (Armoricans and Burgundians).
Theodoric, King and overall commander of the Visigoths.
Thorismund, Theodoric's son and commander of the Visigoth cavalry contingent that seized the hill.
Sangiban, King of the Alans and perhaps sympathetic to his Hunnic cousins.
Meovech, King of the Salian Franks (could belong to Aetius' command).
And on the Hunnic side.
Attila, King of the Huns and commander-in-chief.
Valamir, Theodemir and **Videmir** who jointly command the Ostrogoths — probably best to roll these into one player-character (I know these names sound straight out of Asterix but I didn't make them up, honest!).
Adaric, King of the Gepids who later led the German revolt against the Huns.
The contingents of Thuringians and Ripuarian Franks can also be controlled by different players or included in one of the above commands. We do not know the names of their leaders.

SKIRMISH GAMES

One of the greatest attractions of the Barbarian Invasions as a period for wargaming is the fact that so many of the engagements fought were skirmishes, involving small numbers of troops and a variety of conflicting interests. This means that it is not necessary to amass hundreds of figures to begin wargaming in the period. Additionally, there is great scope for introducing varied scenarios with elements of role-playing adding interest to the game.

What follows is a complete scenario for a skirmish/role-playing

The Victores Iuniores, Auxilium Palatinum. This unit is typical of the small mobile infant units of the field army. They wear no armour and fight primarily with light missile weapons. Protection is derived from the large, colourfully painted shield.

game called *Warlords and Rebels*. It is set in France in the 5th Century. The game involves up to eight players and a game master/umpire. (GM). There is one general briefing which all players receive, as well as individual briefings. I have run this game several times using between three and eight players. If less than eight players are available, the GM can control the lesser characters. Three is probably the minimum number for it to be successful. I use my own *Comitatus* Rules (see Chapter 5) to resolve the action on table but you could use any rules you like as long as they are quick and simple. Complicated rules systems might work with set piece battles but will detract from roleplaying skirmishes such as this. One easy way to resolve action on the table top is for the GM to make subjective decisions, perhaps aided by a percentile die. He may decide, for example that a given attack has a 50% chance of success and roll a percentile die to see if it works. This is clear and quick and allows the action to flow smoothly. The players will only need a sequence of play and perhaps move distances.

The most important, and fun, aspect of this game is the diplomacy and interaction between players. The GM will have to ensure that he makes sufficient provision for this.

This game is a very good introduction to the confused situation in 5th Century France. Not all is as it seems — 'Romans' turns out to be 'barbarians' and supposed enemies turn out to be friends. The GM should keep the identity of troops to himself, thus when a band of nondescript soldiers appear to cries of 'what are they?' he should reply 'what do they look like?' The fact that so many troops would appear identical can add very real command and control problems that no doubt would have plagued the generals of that time.

WARLORDS & REBELS

General Scenario (given to all players)
This game represents the kind of warfare that was common in France in the 5th Century AD as the Roman Empire in the West collapsed. The players all represent generals who have a number of units under their command. They are trying to achieve personal goals and defeat their rivals — just like the historical generals of the time.

The setting is south western France about 440 AD. The country is in turmoil with a Visigothic Kingdom established in the south and making inroads against Roman territory. In Roman-controlled areas, large independent landlords control the countryside with private armies. Small farmers have been driven to seek the protection of these landlords by the insecurity of the region and the crushing burden of taxes which many landlords are strong enough to ignore. Many farmers, slaves, poor and dispossessed have gone into open rebellion and scour the countryside in armed bands called *bacaudae*.

The Count Aetius is trying to restore order. The Rhine frontier has collapsed, the *bacaudae* are active everywhere and the Goths are raiding across the border. At the moment, Aetius is enrolling Hun mercenaries to restore order.

In this particular game, a strong band of Goths has been raiding in the area and Aetius has sent a Roman field army to try to hunt them down. There is a small fort in the region (not on the table), garrisoned by local men who do their best to keep the peace. The real power, however, is the rich landowner Johannes Castius, a personal friend of Count Aetius. Castius has been oppressing his peasants and resisting all attempts by the local authorities to collect taxes from him or to restrain the excesses of his ill-disciplined private army. *Bacaudae* have been seen in the region and have some sympathisers among the local villagers.

Map of the game area (given to all players)

This sketch map shows the general layout of the playing area. The villa is fortified and the river is a major obstacle, crossable

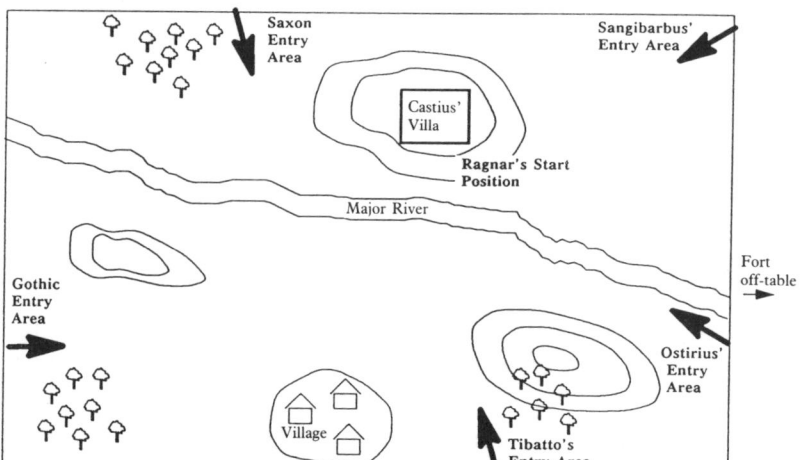

only at fords which are known to the locals but must be found by outsiders.

Individual Briefings

These are kept secret. The troops assigned to each commander are fairly arbitrary and based mostly on the figures I have available. They can easily be adjusted to suit other players as long as they are roughly in the same proportion. Nationalities can also be changed. The Saxon Gundar could, for example, become another Goth if more cavalry than infantry figures are available.

Theodoric's Scenario You are Theodoric, an experienced Visigothic warleader with a reputation for skill and luck. You have been raiding Roman territory for the past few months, dodging Roman Field Armies and their Hun mercenaries. It is almost time to head for home, but first, one more raid. The area you have picked contains a Legionary fort, a rich walled villa and a small village. The fort is too strong to capture, although there is little to fear from the garrison in the open — they are typical Romans, afraid to meet valiant warriors in open battle! The village will be easy but not likely to yield much loot, perhaps only a few slaves and livestock. The villa, on the other hand, is rumoured to be one of the wealthiest in France, but it is well protected.

You have under your comand:

Your Comitatus (bodyguard): armoured cavalry of the highest quality who will follow you to the death. This is the only actual 'unit' you control. The remainder of your army is controlled through subordinates.

Atulf. An old wise warrior who commands his own *comitatus* of cavalry as well as an infantry unit, two archer units and the baggage train (now laden with loot).

Dietric. A young firebrand anxious to make a name for himself but a good warrior. He commands two cavalry units in addition to his own *comitatus*.

Saxons. You have arranged a rendezvous with a Saxon king — Gundar. He will help you fight any Romans in exchange for

Tibatto's bacaudae join forces with the locals to defend the village.

a share of the loot you capture. You might need his help if the Roman Field Army shows up. You don't mind giving him a cut.

Your Objective: Raid at least one target and get back safely.

Victory Points: (cumulative)

Loot villa	100 points
Loot village	50 points
Each archer unit lost	– 5 points
Infantry unit lost	– 10 points
Cavalry unit lost	– 25 points
Baggage train lost	– 100 points
Saxons lost	who cares!

Before the game begins, brief Dietric and Atulf and decide on your plan. You do not know when or where the Saxons will arrive.

Atulf's Scenario (*Note: this character can be controlled by Theodoric if not enough players*) You are Atulf an experienced Visigothic warleader. You have joined forces with Theodoric and Dietric, and have spent the better part of the summer raiding Roman territory and dodging Roman Field Armies and their Hun mercenaries. It is now time to head for home, but unfortunately Dietric is not satisfied and has convinced Theodoric that one more raid is in order. The area they have picked contains a Legionary fort, a rich walled villa and a small village. The fort is too strong to capture, although there is little to fear from the garrison in the open. The village will be easy but not likely to yield much loot, perhaps only a few slaves and livestock. The villa, on the other hand, is rumoured to be one of the wealthiest in France, but it is well protected.

You have under your command:

Your Comitatus (bodyguard): armoured cavalry of the highest quality who will follow you to the death.

One Infantry unit of spearmen, a mix of Gallo-Romans and poorer Goths who are fairly good on the defensive but not great shock troops.

Two Archer units of average quality, unarmoured and not able to stand up in hand-to-hand combat.

The baggage train containing all the loot of your campaign.

Your Objective: Avoid getting bogged down in a hard fight. You want to get your men safely home and don't think any extra loot is worth the risk. You will, however, never desert Theodoric since you have sworn to follow him.

Victory Points: Your reputation is more important than loot or your life. You start the Game with 50 points modified as follows:

Each archer unit lost	– 10 points
Each other unit lost	– 25 points
If Theodoric dies and you survive	– 25 points
If you die fighting after 2 units lost	+ 50 points
If you defeat an enemy leader in combat	+ 10 points
If any additional loot gathered	+ 10 points

Dietric's Scenario You are Dietric a young, brave, Visigothic warleader. You have been raiding Roman territory for the past few months, dodging Roman Field Armies and their Hun mercenaries. Theodoric, your leader, is showing signs of wanting to head for home — encouraged by that old fool Atulf who commands the infantry. You want to gain more riches and increase your reputation. The area you have picked contains a Legionary fort, a rich walled villa and a small village. The fort is too strong to capture, although there is little to fear from the garrison in the open — they are typical Romans, afraid to meet valiant warriors in open battle! The village will be easy but not likely to yield much loot, perhaps only a few slaves and livestock. The villa, on the other hand, is rumoured to be one of the wealthiest in France, it is well protected but not impossible for brave warriors such as you command.

You have under your command:

Your Comitatus (bodyguard): armoured cavalry of the best quality

Two additional units of good Gothic cavalry.

Gundar, the Saxon King, and his *Comitatus* ready to wrest concessions from the Romans in exchange for military service.

Your Objective is to get as much loot as possible, in particular you want to get that villa.

Victory points:

Raid villa only	75 points
Raid villa and village	100 points
Raid village only	0 points
Defeat any enemy leader in personal combat	+25

You have heard rumours that some Saxons may be trying to get a piece of the action, you must try to prevent this.

Gundar's Scenario (Note: this character could be controlled by the GM if not enough players) You are a Saxon king and have been plundering the coast of France for the past few months. You have found the pickings slim and so have headed inland. You met up with Theodoric, a Visigoth, and discussed with him the possibility of raiding a wealthy Roman villa nearby. In the same area there is a Legionary fort and a village. The fort is too strong to take but the garrison is too weak to challenge you in open battle. After doing a reconnaissance of the area you have learned that the villa is well defended by a private army commanded by Ragnar, a Frank. Ragnar is having difficulties with the local villagers and *bacaudae*. He might be willing to make a deal in exchange for your help. Also of interest is the fact that the local Roman military commander (Ostirus) wants to crush Ragnar and force the villa's owner (Castius) to pay his taxes.

Clearly there are opportunities to be made here and you want to secure the best deal for yourself. You really do not care with whom you side. It would be nice to secure a cushy job as a settled ally of the Romans in sunny southern France — beats sailing the North Sea any day!

You have under your command your *Comitatus* (bodyguard) of picked warriors and two units of excellent Saxon infantry.

Your Objective is to secure the best deal for yourself as possible.

Gothic Cavalry charge home on the Roman Infantry line at the Battle of Adrianople.

Victory Points:

Loot the villa with the Goths	25 points
Loot the villa by yourself	50 points
Loot the village	10 points
Obtain land to settle	100 points
Paid cash to leave area	25 points
Each unit lost	– 20 points

You may enter the table whenever you wish. You are in communication with Theodoric, Ragnar and Ostirus. You may send messages through the game master to any of these characters.

Sangibarbus' Scenario (Note: this character could be controlled by the GM if not enough players) You are Sangibarbus, an Alan. You are presently working for the Roman General Aetius. He has charged you with keeping order in southwestern France while he campaigns on the Rhine Frontier. Your main task is to crush any rebellion of *bacaudae* but you are also to keep an eye on the Visigoths.

Tibatto, self-proclaimed king of the *bacaudae,* has been seen in the vicinity of the villa of Johannes Castius. Castius is a friend of Aetius, your boss, so it would be in your interests to keep him happy. Visigothic raiders are also supposed to be in the region.

You have under your command:

Your Comitatus (bodyguard) of trustworthy Alans. Very high morale and devoted to you. They are mounted archers.

Two units of Huns Not bad fellows, similar to your Alans but perhaps not quite as good fighters. Also horse archers.

One unit of Romans — *Equites Catafractarii* Armoured lancers recruited from Sarmatian settlers who are related to the Alans, therefore they are not as useless as most Romans. At least you speak the same language.

Your Objective is to crush any *bacaudae* found in the region. You can make a deal with any Goths you meet, it's the *bacaudae* you are after, not Goths.

Victory Points:

Destroy all *bacaudae* found	50 points
Kill Tibatto	+25 points
Any loot or cash payments	+10 points
Castius makes bad report to Aetius	−10 points
Each unit lost	−10 points
Punish any *bacaudae* sympathisers	+10 points

Ostirus' Scenario You are commander of the fort and responsible for the peace and well being of the area. Barbarian raiders are about and local intelligence indicates they are contemplating an attack. You have notified higher authorities of this and word has reached you that Count Aetius has dispatched a Roman Field Army. You have also had trouble with Johannes Castius the local landowner. Some of his thugs raped one of the village women and the villagers want revenge. They have asked you for justice but you have no legal authority over Castius. In fact the civil authorities have been unable to collect taxes from him. Any action you take against Castius is dangerous, as he is a personal friend of Aetius and he has a strong private army. On the other hand, if you do nothing the villagers might rebel causing your garrison to do the same as they are mostly local men.

A Saxon chief, Gundar, is also roaming the area but fortunately he is less interested in plunder than land to settle. He has contacted you and seems willing to fight for you if the price is right. Unfortunately, unless you seize Castius's estates you have nothing to offer him as you have no money and control no land.

You have under your command

Your Comitatus (bodyguard) of armoured cavalry recruited from Christianized Goths and Huns. Absolutely loyal to you. Armoured horse archers.

Two Cohorts of Legionaries. Poor quality local farmers.

Artillery. Light man-portable bolt throwers, manned by locals.

Two units of Scouts. Better troops than the infantry, light skirmishers who know the countryside. Mostly locals but a few mercenaries as well.

Your Objective: Do what you can to maintain the peace. You must keep the loyalty of your troops and to do this the villagers will have to be avenged. The legal system will not help you if it becomes known that you took it upon yourself to do something about Castius — Aetius would probably have you killed.

Victory Points:

You get rid of Castius	100 points
Your troops rebel	− 50 points
The village is destroyed	− 25 points
You offer cash to the Saxon or any other barbarian	− 10 points
You give the Saxon land to settle	− 20 points
Your troops directly attack Castius or other Romans	− 50 points
Any loot or cash gained for your private funds	+ 10 points

Ragnar's Scenario You are Ragnar, a Frank. You command the private army of Johannes Castius, a powerful Roman landowner. The man is selfish and arrogant but he pays well. Castius has placed you on alert as there has been trouble with the villagers and there are rumours of *bacaudae* raiders in the area. One of your men raped a village woman a few days ago. You had arrested him but Castius ordered him released. You are not happy as you suspect the villagers will rise against you and blame you, not Castius, for the crime. Julius Ostirus is also upset about the incident. Castius tells you not to worry, but you feel that something very serious is brewing.

Interestingly, Gundar, a Saxon king, is raiding nearby and has been in contact with you. He is looking for land to settle in France. He has some excellent warriors with him and might be able to get you out of this bind.

You have under your command:

Your Comitatus (bodyguard). All good Franks like yourself. Reliable and loyal to you alone. Armoured cavalry with spears and javelins.

Two units of Infantry. A mix of mercenaries and ruffians from all over — Goths, Gallo-Romans, Alamanni and Britons. It was one of these who committed the crime. Not particularly loyal or reliable. Unarmoured infantry with javelins.

One unit of archers. Similar to the infantry but a bit more reliable. Armed with bows, swords and shields.

Your Objective is to try to defuse the situation and avoid conflict. Failing that, get the best deal for yourself that you can. You are quite prepared to sacrifice Castius or even your own men (except of course the loyal *comitatus*) if need be.

Victory Points:

End the game with secure employment	100 points
Become involved in combat of any sort	– 25 points
If the villa is looted by any others	– 50 points
Any personal loot or cash payments you get	+ 10 points
If you have to give something up to Gundar	– 10 points

Tibatto's Scenario You are Tibatto, King of the *bacaudae*. The *bacaudae* are farmers, adventurers, escaped slaves and deserters who have banded together to live a free life, independent of Roman or barbarian overlordship. Your power has been growing and you are nearly strong enough to challenge Roman armies in open battle — but not just yet. First you must increase your base of support and recruit new fighters.

This particular area seems a perfect target. The local landowner, Johannes Castius, is hated by the local villagers and local authorities. He maintains a strong private army and lives in a walled villa. One of his thugs recently raped one of the village women and the villagers want revenge. This is also affecting the garrison of the nearby fort since they come from the same village.

Barbarian warbands are roaming the area, Goths, Saxons and Huns. So you will have to be careful. You do not know, however, if they will be hostile or friendly to you. You are fairly sure that you can win over the villagers and subvert the fort's garrison. Julius Ostirus, the fort's commander, is a decent well-meaning man and your spies report that he would very much like to get rid of Castius.

You have under your command:

Your Comitatus (bodyguard) of cavalry. Ex-Roman soldiers for the most part, equipped with javelins.

One unit of fighters. Well equipped men with a high proportion of Roman deserters and German warriors.

One unit of rabble. Escaped slaves and farmers with improvised weapons. Not overly reliable and given to a tendency to loot.

Your Objective is to win the support of the village and gain new recruits.

Victory Points:

If the village is not looted and is sympathetic to you 75 points
Each 'stand' of new recruits with fighting
  experience   + 25 points
Each 'stand' of other new recruits   + 10 points
Each of your units lost   – 50 points

4 PAPER AND PENCIL GAMES

COMMITTEE GAMES

Committee games involve getting a group of players to arrive at a decision or series of decisions. They are quick and easy to run and can be a great deal of fun. Often a committee game will take the form of players taking on roles in a council of war. The scenario is usually devised by a gamemaster who can throw in the odd twist or provide additional information as the game develops. These games can be played in isolation or linked to a battle with miniatures. For example, you could run a council of war between players to decide the order of march for any army and then employ that decision in a battle with or without figures.

Adrianople Committee Game

What follows is a scenario for a committee game based on a real council of war held between the Emperor Valens and his commanders prior to the battle of Adrianople at which they decided to attack immediately without waiting for reinforcements from the West. This council is reported in some detail by Ammianus Marcellinus. To remove the benefit of hindsight, it will be disguised as a council between Julian and his officers prior to Strasbourg, as was previously suggested for a miniatures game on the same subject.

Players take on the following historical roles:

Valens. Emperor of the East who called a council of war to canvass his senior officers for their opinion as to whether he should attack immediately or wait for reinforcements from the West. He was intensely jealous of the fame of Gratian, the Western Emperor, who had just won a victory over the Alamanni, and he wanted to do something that would increase his stature.

Sebastian. Popular commander of infantry who had his eye on the throne. In the historical council he was the leader of those who convinced Valens to attack.

Victor. A Sarmatian who commanded the cavalry. He was prudent and cautious and advised Valens to wait for reinforcements.

Richomer. Count of the household troops who had been sent by Gratian with a letter saying that Gratian would soon be there and urging Valens to 'share the danger and not rashly commit himself to the risks of decisive action single-handed'.

Equitius. Kinsman of Valens and Marshal of the Court. We do not know what advice he gave but he later offered to go to the Goths as a hostage so we can assume he belonged to the cautious camp.

Cassio and Bacurius. Two junior officers who commanded the archers and Scutarii cavalry of the advance guard. They rashly attacked the Goths without orders, forcing the battle to be fought. Perhaps they were ordered to do so by Sebastian when he saw that those wanting to negotiate with the Goths and wait for reinforcements were getting the upper hand. Bacurius was Spanish.

Trajan. Previously commander of infantry but replaced by Sebastian after criticizing Valens so we can assume he belonged to the cautious party.

Valerian. All we know about him is that he died in the battle.

Potentius. A junior cavalry commander but highly respected and son of the former commander-in-chief of the army. We do not know where he stood.

Saturnius. A senior cavalry commander who survived the battle. We do not know his opinion at the council.

The Council of advisors is made up of at least 4 players (Sebastian, Victor and Richomer, Trajan and one of either Cassio or Bacurius) and is divided into two parties; the rash party led by Sebastian who will push Valens to attack, and the cautious party led by Victor who urge him to wait. All the characters are historical, although we only know for certain that Sebastian, Victor and Richomer were present. There is no upper limit on the number of players, and the more there are, the more interesting the discussion will be. Fictional characters can be added if need be. For the game to go well, the councillors should be roughly equally divided in opinion.

The game is played by the gamemaster (GM) giving the players their initial briefings. The information provided to them is purposefully limited, reflecting the actual situation. The army's scouting was very poor as the Gothic army was reported to number only 10,000 when in fact there were considerably more. The Ostrogoth and Alan cavalry were not discovered at all. Valens (in the guise of Julian) convenes and chairs the council and the other players give him their advice when asked for, remembering to be properly circumspect. At the end of discussion (which can be allowed to reach a natural end or be imposed by the GM) Valens will make his decision and then the GM will reveal the true scenario. The aim is to give players some insight into the difficulty of reaching command decisions. It is very easy for us to criticise Valens for acting rashly (and most historians from Ammianus to the 20th Century are critical) but would we have done different in a similar situation?

During the game the GM will introduce delegations from the Goths (calling them Germans) at an appropriate moment. In the historical council there were two delegations, the first one said that the Goths only wanted land to settle and that they had no hostile intentions, he addressed Valens as 'future friend and associate'. A second delegation came later, after the Roman troops had begun to march. Again they offered peace and suggested an exchange of hostages and face to face negotiation between the two leaders. The GM should also be prepared to answer questions from the players and perhaps provide information on troop movements, scouting reports etc. (which he can make up as he goes along). The GM must strive to keep discussion lively and interesting and part of that will be accomplished by assigning players roles that best suit their personalities.

Suggested briefings for the players follow, these can easily be elaborated on by the GM.

General briefing given to all players (disguised to hide the scenario)
You are in France circa 350 AD. The Caesar Julian has recently arrived to take command. He has never before been in battle, up to now he has spent most of his life studying philosophy in Athens. You have received word that a party of Germans have crossed into Roman territory with their families, apparently in-

tending to settle permanently. Your scouts have reported that there are about 10,000 warriors, mostly infantry. You have over 20,000 troops in your army, primarily élite *Palatini* from the Field Army.

Valens' briefing (disguised as if he were the Caesar Julian).
You are the Caesar Julian responsible for the defence of France. You are new to military command and it is very important that you make a name for yourself with the troops and increase your reputation. The Emperor Constantius has been successfully campaigning in the East. He is jealous of you and has been undermining everything you have tried to do. He has said that you are not capable of dealing with such a military problem as this and consequently has dispatched troops under one of his generals to deal with this barbarian incursion. You have to decide whether you will wait for Constantius, thereby risking losing credibility in the eyes of your soldiers, or attack now and secure fame for yourself.

Your inclination is to attack now before Constantius' troops come and take all the glory, but being a prudent man you have called a council of your senior officers to ask their advice. After you have listened to all you want, you will make your decision.

Your staff consists of:

Sebastian, your best officer. An excellent tactician and very popular with the troops. He has recently replaced Trajan as *Magister Peditum* (Master of Infantry).

Victor, a Sarmatian and known for his cautious approach. He is *Magister Equitum* (Master of Cavalry).

Richomer, *Magister Officiorum* (Master of Offices) who commands the household troops of the Emperor Constantius. He has come from Constantius with a message telling you in part to 'share the danger and not rashly commit yourself to the risks of decisive action single-handed'.

Trajan, formerly *Magister Peditum* but you had him replaced by Sebastian because he was lazy, incompetent and critical of yourself. He is dangerous and probably has his eye on the throne.

Equitius, a kinsman of yours and *Curator Palatii* (Marshal of the Court). He has a high sense of honour and you respect him, he is the highest ranking official present after yourself but is a civilian with only limited military experience.

Potentius, a junior cavalry commander but highly respected and son of the former commander-in-chief of the army.

Saturnius, a senior cavalry commander.

Valerian, Cassio and *Bacurius.* Junior officers.

Your aim is to make the best decision possible to advance your career and deal with the threat.

Sebastian's briefing
You are Sebastian, *Magister Peditum* (Master of Infantry) of Julian's army. You are a capable, seasoned officer and very popular with the troops. You are without a doubt the best commander on Julian's staff and what you say carries a lot of weight, Cassio and Bacurius will follow whatever you say. Trajan is your enemy as he was previously *Magister Peditum* but was removed from office and replaced by you.

Your aim is to get Julian to attack the barbarians now. If he does, you will probably gain a great deal of credit for victory, as it is well known that you are his best general. If he waits, Constantius' general will steal the glory.

Victor's briefing
You are *Magister Equitum* (Master of Cavalry) and equal in rank to Sebastian. Together you are the senior army commanders. You don't like this situation. You think that the barbarians pose no pressing threat and you would be better off to wait for reinforcements to make certain of victory. Your aim is to convince Julian to wait.

Richomer's briefing
You are *Magister Officiorum* (Master of Offices), commander of the Imperial Household troops, sent by the Emperor Constantius to tell Julian that he should wait for reinforcements. Personally you think Constantius is just jealous of Julian as the barbarians don't seem so strong. For political reasons you must convey Constantius' message and be cautious of contradicting him. Your aim is to give Julian the best advice you can without dam-

aging your standing with Constantius.

Trajan's briefing
You used to be commander of the infantry but Julian replaced you with Sebastian when he arrived in France after it was reported that you were critical of him. Your aim is to discredit Sebastian, you don't really care whether Julian attacks now or waits.

Equitius' briefing
You are *Curator Palatii* (Marshal of the court) the highest ranking official here after the Caesar. You are a civilian with only limited military experience. You are very conscious of your position and feel yourself above this military riffraff (especially barbarians like Sebastian, Richomer and Victor). It seems more prudent to wait for reinforcements but you will advise whatever seems honourable to you and try to impress Julian.

Potentius' briefing.
You are a junior cavalry officer but from a very noble family which adds weight to your opinion. You want to attack now and get the battle over with. If you wait for reinforcements the barbarians might do untold damage.

Cassio and Bacurius (identical briefings)
You are a junior officer and your opinions will not carry that much weight. You are a client of Sebastian and will support him in whatever he does (but don't make it too obvious).

Valerian's briefing
You are a junior officer and your opinions will not carry that much weight. You are a client of Victor and will support him in whatever he does (but don't make it too obvious).

Saturnius' briefing
You are a senior cavalry officer with a lot of experience on the frontier. You are not convinced that a victory is guaranteed if you attack now. There may be more barbarians than your scouts reported and there is no harm in waiting for more troops to ensure victory. Personally you suspect that Julian (and Sebastian his right hand man) are more interested in glory than a military success.

CAMPAIGNS

A campaign is a means of linking tabletop battles together and including strategic and non-military considerations into wargames. There are numerous possibilities for interesting campaigns set in this period, particularly as there were so many competing groups and no single dominant faction. The most interesting campaigns contain role-playing elements, casting players in the roles of kings, generals or emperors. Interaction between the players is a major element of the game. Such campaigns can easily be played by post with players writing in their 'orders' to the gamemaster who will then determine the outcome of the various player actions and resolve resulting conflicts. Setting up a detailed campaign is a great deal of work for the gamemaster and requires a major commitment of time. It may be better to proceed slowly, perhaps with a simple two player campaign where the battles fought with figures are loosely linked together in a historical setting. Alternatively a boardgame could be used to determine strategic moves, while tactical moves are resolved using figures.

Britain, 5th Century AD

A fairly simple and very interesting campaign could be set in Britain after the withdrawal of the Roman troops. Players could represent Picts, Scots, Saxons, and the numerous Romano-British warleaders. This is an ideal setting for a campaign as armies were small (often only in the hundreds), alliances were varied and external influences were few since the island was cut off from the mainstream of events on the continent. This last factor is particularly important if you want to develop a simple campaign because you do not need to deal with events on the periphery.

Stilicho and Alaric

A good two player campaign could be built around the struggle between Stilicho and Alaric for control of Italy between 401 and 410 AD. The armies of these two warlords were equal in strength and fairly similar in composition. Alaric, a Visigoth, had been appointed commander of the army of modern day Yugoslavia (*magister militum per Illyricum*) and would have been able to supply his followers from the Roman logistical system. His army would have also included units of the Roman army as well as adventurers, brigands and warriors from other tribes. Stilicho was the commander of the Western armies but he relied heavily

The Count Aetius in the 5th Century with his personal bodyguard of Huns.

on Alans and other Visigoths (commanded by Sarus, an enemy of Alaric's).

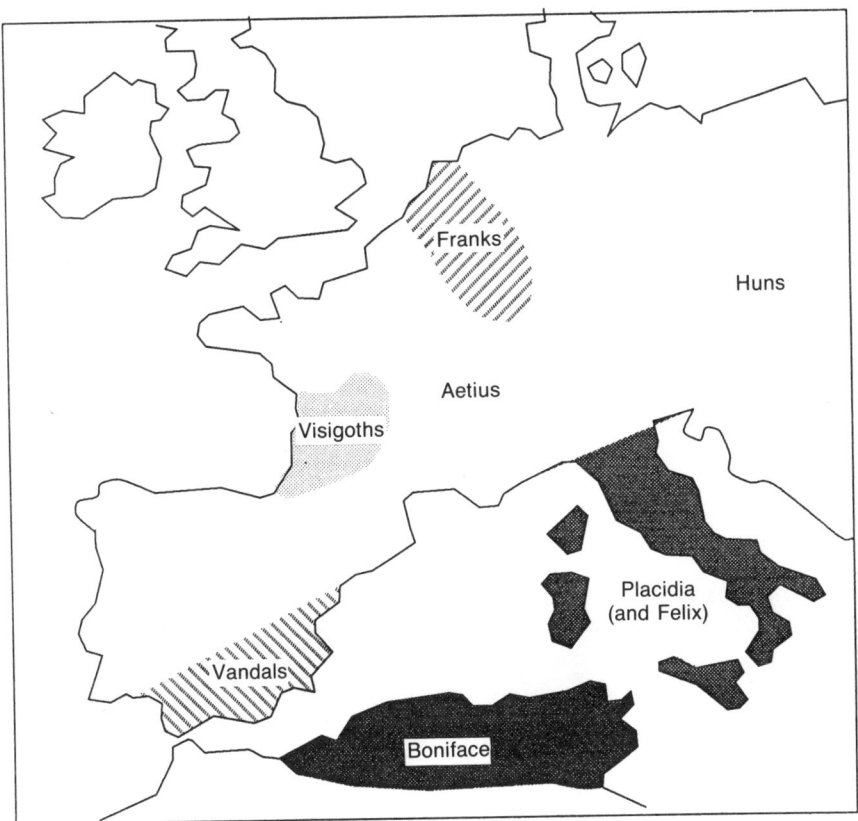

This map shows the major power centres for a possible Campaign in the West at about 425 AD.

Struggle for the West, 425 AD

A more complicated multi-player campaign could ideally be situated in the West at about 425 AD. At this time there was a major power struggle going on for control of the West Roman armies between Aetius (based in France) and Boniface (based in Africa). The various barbarian kingdoms — Vandals, Visigoths and Franks — were strong enough to challenge these generals or at least influence events. On the periphery you have the East Roman Empire and the Huns who could also come into play.

Major characters for such a campaign would be:

Aetius. Commander of the army in France. He had developed a friendship with Rua, King of the Huns, (this is prior to Attila) and relied on Huns to form the backbone of his army.

Boniface. Commander of the Army in Africa, favoured by the Empress Galla Placidia over Aetius.

Galla Placidia. Mother of Valentinian III, a child emperor. She controls the Western Imperial Court (at Ravenna) and has appointed Felix as her top general. Felix controls the Army of Italy.

Gaiseric. King of the Vandals in Spain who later crossed into Africa, defeated Boniface and seized the province for himself.

Theodoric. King of the Visigoths settled in southwestern France and frequently in conflict with Aetius.

Chlodio. King of the Franks on the lower Rhine frontier.

Rua. King of the Huns, still favourably disposed towards the West Romans and supplying Aetius with troops.

Theodosius II. Emperor of the East who does not seem to interfere very much in events in the West.

Such a campaign would be a major undertaking involving several players and a gamemaster/umpire to bring it all together.

5 COMITATUS: RULES FOR MINIATURES GAMES

INTRODUCTION

What follows are some basic rules for playing games with miniatures in this period, which I call *Comitatus*. They have been derived from *Legio*, complete rules that I have developed for fighting battles in the Roman era. These rules, while complete, are not all-inclusive. They provide players with a starting point and some general concepts that could be further developed. When in doubt on any point, use common sense.

The game is played using alternate movement, with turns broken down into phases. The sequence of play is derived from Ammianus Marcellinus' descriptions of battle. After deployment into Battle Formation, troops move to within bow range of each other. They must then halt and exchange missiles at long range. Troops then close to within javelin range, again exchange missiles, then close to combat. Once combat is joined the lines will sway back and forth until one side becomes worn down and breaks. A charge in the flank or rear will often settle the combat.

There are two movement phases per turn. This allows troops beyond bow range of the enemy to move further each turn, reflecting the fact that they need not behave as cautiously.

Since morale decreases as combat is prolonged, it pays to have a reserve of fresh troops who can intervene at a critical moment, just as the *Legio Primani* did at the Battle of Strasbourg.

Once joined, combat is not necessarily continuous. After fighting for a number of turns with no result, troops will mutually separate for a breathing space.

Key Elements for Rules

Any rules covering this period should take into account certain characteristics, most important among these are the command and control relationships. Battles were often fought between warlords pursuing their special interests, backed by their loyal *Comitatus*. The way I have approached these rules, therefore, is to break the battle down into the phases described above and integrate a certain amount of characterization, whereby player-characters will have to personally intervene to encourage troops to take certain actions. Descriptions of battle by Ammianus and Procopius make it clear that weapons and armour were not the deciding factors in battle, rather it was personal leadership and the morale of the troops. These rules, therefore, play down the subtle differences in equipment and use simple combat mechanisms. This allows the emphasis to be placed on morale and leadership.

These rules use the standard 6 x 4cm or 6 x 6cm stands, described in Chapter 2, as the basic playing piece. The actual number of figures on each stand does not matter.

RULES

Command

1. Players play the role of a commander represented on the table by a command figure surrounded by his *Comitatus* (called a 'Command Stand').

2. These command stands each have 1-3 **Control Points (CP)** and 1-3 **Inspiration Points (IP)** (these can be assigned arbitrarily, by dice, or based on a historical character). These points indicate how well a player-character can control or inspire his troops (the higher the better). A **Control Radius** is derived from the Control Points: 1 = 6 cm radius; 2 = 12 cm radius; 3 = 18 cm radius. Only troops within the command stand's control radius can be controlled by the player (see 27b).

3. Control Points will assist in determining when players move in the order of play. They also indicate the number of command options available each turn. At the start of each turn there is a command phase in which players may expend up to their maximum allotment of CPs to carry out various command options (see 27).

4. Inspiration Points only affect troops with 6cm of the command stand. These points are used to temporarily raise the morale of troops within 6cm to encourage them to close with the enemy, to charge, to encourage them in combat, or to rally from rout.

Organization

5. Troops are organized into units of 1-6 stands of either

Infantry, Cavalry or Skirmishers. Fighting abilities are determined by the **Attack, Defence and Missile Factors** given in paragraph 9 below.

6. Units are organized into commands of either Infantry or Cavalry, which may also include some Skirmish units. A command is led by a commander who is represented on table by a command stand. A commander-in-chief commands the entire army.

7. Each unit has a **Unit Effectiveness Rating (UER)**. This is a numerical rating that measures the overall combat effectiveness of the unit, based on morale and fatigue. The UER will be modified due to events experienced. Initial UER is derived from the morale of the troops as follows:

poor morale =	1 + die roll
average morale =	3 + die roll
high morale =	5 + die roll
exceptional morale =	7 + die roll

8. The sample armies described in Chapter 2 give an idea of appropriate levels of morale for various troop types.

Troop Types

9. The following list gives sample troop types, classifying them as Cavalry, Infantry or Skirmishers, and listing their Attack **(A)**, Defence **(D)**, Short Range Missile **(S)** and Long Range Missile **(L)** Factors. A missile factor of ' – ' means those troops have no weapon usable at that range. A factor of '**0**' means those troops have low effect, which can be modified. More detailed descriptions of the troops can be found in Chapter 2.

Cavalry

German Cavalry. A4/D1/S2/L – . All German Cavalry. The Vandals and similar, who did not use javelins, would have no Short Range Factor; Alamannic cavalry mixed with infantry would increase their defence factor by '1' and count as a deeper formation in calculating 'advantage' (see 32d).

Steppe Light Cavalry. A2/D0/S3/L2. Horse Archers of the Huns and Alans. Probably also equipped with swords, shields, lassoes and possibly spears.

Steppe Heavy Cavalry. A4/D1/S3/L2. Sarmatians and the small number of Hun and Alan nobles who may have fought as shock cavalry.

Light Javelin Cavalry. A2/D1/S4/L –. Roman, Celtic, Pictish and Moorish light javelin-armed cavalry.

Roman Heavy Cavalry. A3/D2/S3.L –. Conventional Roman cavalry, including Romano-British and Gallo-Romans.

Roman Horse Archers. A1/D0/S3/L2. Light bow armed cavalry.

Heavy Horse Archers. A2/D2/S3/L2. Well armoured Roman Horse Archers, probably of Hunnic origin, who were introduced by Aetius and later became the mainstay of East Roman Armies. This category also includes bow-armed *Clibanarii*. Élite units also carried spears, increasing the Attack Factor to '3'.

Catafractarii. A4/D1/S – /L –. Heavily armoured cavalry based on the Sarmatians.

Clibanarii. A5/D2/S – /L –. Completely armoured lancers on armoured horses.

Infantry

German Infantry. A3/D2/S1/L1 –. Foot soldiers of all German nations.

Roman Infantry. A2/D3/S3.L –. Includes both Legionaries and Auxiliaries.

Javelinmen. A2/D2/S3/L –. Isuarians, Scots and Welsh.

Picts. A2/D3/S – /L –. Picts armed with long spears. Their favourite formation was a defensive circle. Other Picts may have been javelin or bow-armed skirmishers.

Levied Spearmen. A1/D2/S – /L –. Lesser trained Roman Limitanei, sub-Roman militia, Gallo-Romans and the later infantry of the Goths and Burgundians after the firm establishment of their kingdoms.

Armed Rabble. A1/D1/S1/L –. Armed civilians, including *bacaudae*, equipped with whatever they can find. The hard core *bacaudae* could increase Defence Factor to '2'.

Skirmishers

Foot skirmishers. A2/D1/S5/L –. Light infantry javelinmen or slingers.

Roman Cavalry were more heavily armoured than their infantry counterparts

Archers. A0/D1/S4/L3. Foot archers. Some may have been intended to hold ground and would have been equipped with swords, shields and perhaps helmets. These would increase the Defence Factor to '2'.

Specialists. A0/D1/S4/L4. The very small number of Roman crossbowmen and staff slingers. It is also possible that some Picts and Romano-British had crossbows.

Artillery. A0/D1/S4/L4. Roman light portable bolt throwers. Retains long range factor out to 48cm.

Dice
10. Normal 6 sided dice are used to determine the results of shooting and combat. Roman Field Army troops and all *Comitati* use Average dice (marked: 2, 3, 3, 4, 4, 5) for all other actions. All others use normal 6 sided dice.

Formations
11. Units must be either **Formed** or **Unformed**. An unformed unit is one that is spread out to skirmish or disrupted by some other event. All skirmishers and cavalry (except Cataphracts) may voluntarily become unformed to skirmish, spacing stands about 6cm apart. A formed unit is one that is closed up and acting as a cohesive body.

12. Units are unformed if they:
    a. voluntarily spread out to skirmish.
    b. evade, rout, break-off, pursue.
    c. are recoiled by charging cavalry.
    d. are charged in the flank or rear.

13. Once unformed, a unit must *Rally* to re-form. This is done by re-forming the stands on the officer, facing any desired direction.

14. **Disorder.** A temporary break in unit cohesiveness caused by:
    a. Morale Test.
    b. being unformed.
    c. two HITS per stand in front rank from missile fire.
    d. surprise.
    e. some troops moving through difficult terrain (see 21).

15. Disorder ceases after the Morale Phase, once the cause of Disorder has been removed.

16. **Command Formations.** Units may either be controlled and formed independently, or formed together in one of the following

Command Formations:
   a. *Battle Formation.* 1-2 lines for Romans, 1 line for barbarians. No more than 6cm between units in each line. Some units may skirmish to the front/flank/rear and others may be held in reserve. Skirmishers, rear lines and reserve may be separated by up to 24cm.
   b. *March Column.* All units in a single column, one stand wide, with no more than 6cm between units. Some unformed units may scout to the front/flank and may be separated from the main column by up to 24cm.

17. Units in a Command Formation are moved and controlled as one entity. Independent units (ie. those not in a Command Formation) are moved and controlled individually.

18. Changing Formations:
   a. Independent Units — Battle Formation: Romans 2 units per phase, others 1 unit per phase;
   b. March Column — Battle Formation: Romans 3 units per phase, others 2 units per phase.
   c. The number of units may be increased by one for each CP expended by the commander within command radius.

19. Battle Formation is formed by moving the allowed number of units into position regardless of the distance moved. If any of the units fight or shoot while forming up, they must wait until the next turn.

Movement

20. Movement Rates:
   Formed: 18cm foot; 24cm mounted
   Unformed: 24cm foot; 36cm mounted
   Evade, Rout, Pursuit, Break-off: use unformed move.
   Command in March Column: move 48cm on road, 36cm off road.
   Recoil: 6cm
   Repulse: separate infantry by 6cm, cavalry by 24cm

21. **Terrain Effect:**

Troop Type	Terrain Type		Major Obstacles	Minor
	Rough	Broken		
Skirmishers	–	–	–6cm	–
Infantry	2x(D)	2x	–6(D)	(D)
Cavalry	no	2x(D)	no	–6(D)

Notes: (D) = become disordered; 2x = twice distance; – = no effect; –6 = move reduced by 6cm; no = impassable

A 4th Century Roman army on the wargames table.

Notes on Movement:
Roads/bridges reduce terrain effects to next lower category, ie. Rough to Broken; Minor Obstacle to no Obstacle etc.

Roman auxiliaries prior to 400 AD and all barbarian infantry are not disordered by difficult terrain, although other effects remain.

22. Direction Changes:
    a. Unformed units are moved as individual stands. They may wheel and turn freely with no reductions to movement.
    b. Formed units change direction as indicated in the sequence of play (see 28 & 30).

23. Allowed changes are:
    1) turn to the flank or rear.
    2) change frontage by doubling or halving ranks.
    3) mount or dismount: two mounted stands dismount to form one infantry stand or two skirmisher stands.
    4) incline: move equal distance forwards and sideways (Roman Infantry only).
    5) side-step/step-back: move up to 6cm in either direction counting as full move distance (Roman Infantry only).
    6) wheel: inside edge of unit remains in place while rest wheel forward. Measure furthest distance moved.

24. Interpenetration. Two units may freely interpenetrate if one is stationary, and one is unformed not more than one stand deep. Otherwise both units will become disordered.

Sequence of Play

25. Players move alternately each Phase. To determine who moves first each turn, roll a die and add that player-character's CPs. High score chooses whether to move first or last.

26. Each Phase in the sequence of play is completed by all players before proceeding to the next.

27. Command Phase:
    a. Each Command Stand may expend up to its maximum allotment of CPs doing any of the following (each action takes 1 CP):
        1) control troops within command radius.
        2) move anywhere within 24cm (may move again in movement phases).
        3) issue orders to a subordinate commander, send or listen to a message.

b. Units that are not controlled, either because they are beyond command radius or the commander opted not to use his CPs to control them, must take a control test:
Roll Die: 1-2 = Halt, 3-4 = Act as player wishes;
5-6 = Repeat last move.
+ 1 if in pursuit.

Notes on Command and Control:

To Control troops the command stand must elect to expend a CP, it does not happen automatically just because the troops are within the control radius.

Troops which are controlled may be moved as the player wishes. Units in a Command Formation are controlled as one entity, as long as part of the Formation is within control radius all units may be controlled.

28. March Phase. Only troops further than Long Missile Range (24cm) from the enemy may move in this phase. All moves must end at, or beyond, long range. Troops in rout make a rout move, others may do one of:

a. Move up to full distance.
b. Romans change direction + move up to ½ distance.
c. Others change direction.
d. Rally.
e. Form Battle Formation.

29. Long Range Missile Exchange. Shoot at targets at Long Range (beyond 6cm, up to 24cm).

Procedure:

— Roll two dice per infantry stand, one die for others. − 1/2 if shooting overhead or shot 3 or more times before.
—Result less/equal to Long Range Factor = HIT.
− 1 from Factor for each of: Target unformed skirmishers/cavalry; Target armoured.

Notes on Shooting:

Enemy within 6cm of friends are not eligible as a target.
Overhead shooting. Troops on a higher elevation may shoot, and be shot at, over the heads of others on lower ground. Roman archers attached to an infantry unit may shoot over the heads of that unit, if in base-to-base contact with it.

Gaps must be at least 6cm wide to shoot through.

Ammunition supply is taken into account by halving the number of eligible shooters after three turns of shooting.

Artillery has an unlimited ammunition supply and may shoot out to 48cm.

After exchanging missiles, Romans and Alamanni prepare to close to hand-to-hand combat.

30. Tactical Move Phase. Troops in rout make a rout move. All other troops may do one of the following:
   a. Approach (close to within short range of enemy) if:
      UER + Attack Factor + number of stands = 9 +
      + 1 if skirmishers/cavalry with no Long Range Factor.
      + IPs added by Leader within 6cm.
   b. Unformed skirmishers and cavalry must fall back in face of an Approach by formed enemy to maintain desired skirmishing distance.
   c. Rally or withdraw to beyond long range to Rally next turn.
   d. Form Battle Formation or turn.
   e. Make a March Phase option if remaining beyond long range.

Notes on Tactical Moves:

An Approach move closes the distance from long to short range. It must end at short range (6cm).

Troops who do not meet the requirements for an approach may not move closer to enemy than long range although there is nothing to prevent enemy from approaching them.

If an entire line in Battle Formation is making the Approach, count the number of stands in the line when determining whether the Approach can be made, otherwise count the number of stands in the unit.

Unformed skirmishers and cavalry who must withdraw in face of an enemy approach do so simultaneously with enemy movement.

The only direction changes allowed in this phase are 90 or 180 degree turns.

31. Short Range Missile Exchanges. All troops with a missile factor may shoot at short range (6cm). Others who did not move in the Tactical Phase, and horse archers whether they moved or not, may also shoot at beyond short range using their long range factor.

32. Combat Phase. Simultaneously:
   a. Charge (close from short range to contact) if:
      — Pursuing,
      — or if formed and UER + *Attack Factor* + *number of stands in unit* = 9 +
   b. If Charged, determine Charge Response: *if Die + UER + number of stands in unit, less than 6 = Break.* Otherwise:
      1) Unformed, skirmishers may receive at the halt if in, or separated by, difficult terrain, or if charged by cavalry, otherwise Evade.

2) Unformed cavalry evade.
3) Other cavalry counter-charge.
4) Others receive at the halt.

c. Modify score needed to charge/respond to charge by:

Leader in 6cm	+IPs
Charge flank/rear/disorder	+2
Veterans	+1
Unformed or Column	−2
Cavalry to Charge good order infantry frontally	−2
Raw foot charged by cavalry	−2

d. Resolve Combat between troops in base to base combat by:
1) Determining Advantage. Troops following up a recoil always have advantage as do:
pursuers over routers;
formed over unformed (other than pursuers); and
all troops over unarmed wagons, civilians etc.

Otherwise add:

UER 2+	+1
Advantage of Ground	+1
Advantage of Formation	+1
In Pursuit	+1

— Advantage of Ground = uphill, behind defences, charged downhill or moved downhill prior to charge etc.
— Advantage of Formation = good order over disorder, deeper formation up to a maximum of two stands deep, etc. Infantry stands count twice as deep as Cavalry or Skirmishers.

2) Roll one die per stand in contact. Result less/equal to Attack Factor (Charge, pursue, follow up); Defence Factor (other cases) = HIT.

+2 if Advantage; −1 if Armoured Opponent

Factor cannot be increased to more than 5

e. Results of Combat:
1) Each unit more HITS than inflicted = BREAK if unformed or UER 0 or less. Otherwise recoil 6cm and take a morale test.
3) *Pursuit.* HIT = Stand eliminated.
4) Cavalry who charged Infantry and failed to disorder or break them, are repulsed 24cm.
5) After two consecutive rounds of combat with no recoil/break = Repulse (separation of 6cm between foot, 24cm between mounted or mounted and foot).

Notes on Combat:
In Impact (one or both sides charged) only stands in contact with enemy count. In Mêlée (remaining in contact from previous turn), up to one stand overlapping on each side may be counted in addition.

Charge moves end at contact with enemy or, if the target evade or routed, on the target's original position. The charger is required to pursue evaders/routers except in the circumstances at (34 f). If the pursuers meet new enemy they may either charge in or halt 6cm short. If they charge in this instance, they are considered to be in good order but not in pursuit.

An Evade Move is made unformed in one of the following directions:
— directly away from the charge
— to interpenetrate a friendly unit which it may freely do (see 24)
— to reach difficult terrain or cross an obstacle.

A counter-charge counts as a charge and meets the charger half way.

33. Morale Phase. Working from left to right:
a. Adjust UER for –

Each HIT received	– 1
Charged or Evaded	– 1
Leader killed, wounded, routed	– IPs
Opponent broke, broke-off, eliminated	+ 1
Complete turn spent beyond long range.	+ 1

b. Test Morale if:
Unit lost combat
To cease rout
Friendly unit, other than skirmishers, broke within 24cm

c. Morale test procedure: *if Die + UMR + Stands in unit, less than 6 = Break* if disordered, raw or unsupported; otherwise become disordered. Modify if:

Comitati	+ 1
Leader in 6cm	+ IPs
Enemy behind flank/rear (6cm)	– 1

Notes on Morale:
The increase in UER for each turn spent beyond long range of enemy is to allow units to rest. UER may never be increased to more than 2 points less than the original rating

34. Post Combat Move Phase. Units make recoil, rout, break-off, repulse, follow-up, pursuit moves as required.

a. **Recoil** is a combat result. The entire unit is moved back and must take a morale test. If it cannot move due to blocking troops, impassable terrain etc., it will become unformed.

b. **Rout** is a compulsory unformed move made by a unit that has broken:

1) Initial rout move resulting from combat or morale test is made in this phase. Other and succeeding moves are made during other movement phases. Rout moves are reduced by 6cm for each phase of movement. The move is a straight line away from the enemy who broke them, or nearest threat, then towards the friendly table edge or camp. If the path is blocked, routers will try to move around the blockage. If there is no way around they will halt.
2) Routers will cause all raw and unformed troops with UER 4 or less within 6cm, to break and be swept up in the rout.
3) If the routers' path is blocked by friendly troops they will (in order of priority):
   — Burst through unformed troops causing them to break
   — Head for any gap, at least 6cm wide, within 24cm;
   — Burst through non-infantry, causing them to become unformed.
   — Halt.
4) Routers meeting fresh enemy will attempt to move around them beyond short range. If unable to do this they will halt.
5) Halted routers may recommence movement once the reason for halting is removed.
6) Routers throw away all heavy weapons and shields. As a result all their factors permanently halved (round down).
7) Rout ceases after routers pass a morale test.

c. **Break-off** is a voluntary unformed move to break contact. It may only be conducted by skirmishers or cavalry other than cataphracts. It is conducted as a rout but is only one move. If contacted by pursuers the breakers-off will truly break.

d. Repulsed troops end up facing each other in good order.

Although Germans predominated, auxiliaries from many nations were employed in the Roman army. This unit, *Equites Mauri Feroces*, was recruited from the Moors of North Africa who were excellent light cavalry. Moors were also employed by the Vandals after the establishment of their African kingdom.

e. **Requirement to follow-up/pursue.** Recoils must be followed up, routs and break-offs must be pursued, except in the following cases where it is optional:
- by non-raw Roman infantry.
- by any *Comitati,* or
- if all opponents were unformed skirmishers

f. Follow-up is done by keeping stands in contact. Repulse is not followed up.

g. **Pursuit** is moved in the same way as a rout:
1) If pursuers have a faster movement than routers they will catch them.
2) If routers and pursuers have the same move distance each roll a die. If pursuers roll equal or higher they will catch the routers, otherwise end 6cm behind. *– 1 from score for armoured troops, + 1 for Skirmishers.*
3) Pursuers who meet fresh enemy have the option of moving around them to follow their opponent or halting at short range. Pursuers who halt for this reason may charge the new target next turn even if not normally eligible.
4) Pursuit ceases after the Command Phase if the pursuers are controlled or get a control test result other than 'repeat last move'.

Special Rules

35. *Comitati.* Each commander may have a *comitatus* of as many stands as he has Inspiration Points. The *comitati* would be better armoured and steadier than the normal troops of the same type and, therefore, may have a defence factor one point higher than normal for that troop type. Roman commanders may have barbarian *comitati* but not the other way around. Commanders may temporarily leave their *comitatus.* In this case, the remaining *comitatus* stands may not make any moves except to rejoin their leader or to respond to a charge. Such a separation does not cause the unit to become unformed.

36. *Experience.* Most troops would have an average amount of experience and training. Those troops, however, who have no battle experience or whose training has been neglected, may be classed as 'Raw'. They will be more brittle in combat and generally less steady. *Comitati* will be 'Veterans', as may some units who have been on a long campaign.

A Roman Commander is shown here accompanied by his *Comitatus*. This particular unit is the *Scola Scutariorum Prima* and like most other units of the Roman Army is probably primarily composed of Germans.

37. *Armour.* Only Cataphracts on armoured horses or Infantry in metal armour count as 'armoured'. The only infantry in metal armour would be German Infantry *Comitati* or a few élite Roman Legions.

38. *Challenges.* Personal challenges to combat between leaders was a characteristic of these times. They may be issued by any barbarian commander, or a Roman after 400 AD. A leader may appoint a Champion to fight for him, even if he issues the challenge. If the challenge is issued but not accepted, roll one die for every non-Roman cavalry unit in the army: '6' = a warrior from that unit will accept the challenge, regardless of the commander's intent, and will be treated as a 'champion'.

39. Personal Combat procedure:
— Move stands to a mean point between armies, 6cm apart;
— Simultaneously exchange javelins, 6 = HIT;
— Close to contact, stab with spears, 5-6 = HIT;
— Continue combat with swords, 4-6 = HIT.
— Each HIT causes a wound, reducing ability to HIT by '1' for each wound. Three wounds = Lost Combat. Roll a die. 1-2 = Dead, 3-6 = severely wounded but rescued by his *comitatus*. Lose 1 CP for each wound after the first. No other troops may interfere with the combat.

40. The results of personal combat are:
Challenge not accepted by enemy + 1 UER of all units.
Win Combat + 1 UER of all units, + 1 IP
Lose Combat − 1 UER of all units, − 1 IP (if survived)

41. If a champion fought, the results are the same but no change to IPs.

42. *Pre-Battle Speeches* may be made by the commander-in-chief once the majority of troops are in Battle Formation but before any approaches are made. To do this the player must actually deliver the speech and be judged on its effect by the GM or bystanders. If it is judged to be good, the UER of all troops is raised by '1'; if poor, UER is reduced by '1'; if average, there is no result. This can be most instructive and, of course, entertaining, particularly if the speech draws a large crowd!

APPENDIX
FURTHER READING

This book has only touched the surface of many aspects of the Barbarian Invasions period. Many readers will want to delve further to achieve greater understanding and I recommend the following books as good places to start:

Primary Sources
The Later Roman Empire. Ammianus Marcellinus. Published by Penguin Classics (1986). This is probably the single best introduction to the period. Ammianus was a Roman Officer who lived through the events of the 4th Century which he describes. There is very good detail on the major battles, interesting skirmishes and politics. It is a great book to use to develop a scenario.

History of the Wars. Procopius. Published by the Leob Classical Library. Although a 6th Century writer, Procopius can be used to get a feeling for warfare just beyond this period. He describes the wars between the East Romans and Vandals, Persians and Goths.

The Art of War. Vegitius. This is a military manual written in the 5th Century. It gives invaluable detail on tactics and provides insight into the organization, equipment and morale of the Roman army. It must, however, be used with caution as the writer often confuses reality, wishful thinking and faulty impressions of the past.

Modern Sources
The Armies and Enemies of Imperial Rome, 4th Ed. Phil Barker. Published by the Wargames Research Group (1981). This book gives excellent detail on the organization of the Roman Army together with a look at the dress and equipment of soldiers. Most valuable of all is the inclusion of many parts of the *Notitia*

Dignitatum giving shield designs and deployment of most units of the later Roman Army.

The Fall of the Roman Empire. Arther Ferrill. Published by Thames and Hudson Ltd (1986). A good book that pulls together many aspects of the Fall of Rome but needs to be approached cautiously as many conclusions presented are based on scanty evidence and at times faulty logic.

Novels

I believe that good historical novels have a valid place in furthering one's understanding of a period of history. They should not be used as a means of gathering factual information but rather as a way of getting a 'feel' for a period.

Sword at Sunset. Rosemary Sutcliffe. Hodder & Stoughton Ltd (1963). This, I believe, is the best of the many books written on the legend of King Arthur. It is set in 5th Century Britain and gives a good feel for the time.

The Little Emperors. Alfred Duggan. Faber & Faber Ltd (1951). Set in Britain at the time of the revolt of Constantine (408) and the removal of the last Roman troops. It presents the decline of the social and political structure of the Empire, giving a feeling for the *bacaudic* uprisings and the gradual transfer of power from Roman authorities to local warlords.

The Boat of Fate. Keith Roberts. Century Hutchinson Ltd (1971). This is set in Spain, France and Britain in the 5th Century and gives the reader an excellent appreciation of the difficulties faced by a Roman commander of barbarian federates and again touches on the uprisings of the *bacaudae*.

Eagle in the Snow. Wallace Breem. Sphere Books Ltd (1971). This book focuses on the crossing of the frozen Rhine by the Germans in 406. Many of the details of military organization are wrong but the overall feel of the book is excellent.

Julian. Gore Vidal. Signet Books (1971). The story of the Emperor Julian with excellent detail on the politics and religious problems of the 4th Century. Still in print.

Count Belisarius. Robert Graves. Cassell Publishers Ltd (1939), recently reprinted by Penguin. The story of Belisarius, the East Roman General who re-conquered Africa and Italy in the 6th Century. It is based on Procopius and captures the political and military climate of the period immediately after the Barbarian Invasions. Still in print.

The Society of Ancients

The Society of Ancients devotes itself to the study of military history in the pre-gunpowder era. *Slingshot* is the society journal which is published six times a year and contains a wealth of information on both wargaming and history. The Later Roman Empire and the Barbarian Invasions is often the subject of discussion. The society also has a number of other publications, and sponsors an annual conference. I highly recommend joining if you have any interest in the ancient and medieval periods.

INDEX

Adrianople, Battle of 7, 11, 19, 43-45, 57, 63-68
Aetius 15, 29, 39, 45-47, 50, 70, 72
Alamanni 7, 10, 12, 16, 19, 21, 24, 26, 38, 39, 41, 63, 71
Alans 11, 12, 27, 39, 43, 45, 47
Alaric 11, 69
Ammianus Marcellinus 7, 8, 24, 63, 73, 74, 92
Angon 26
Armoricans (Bretons) 13, 15, 19, 39, 45-47
Armour 24, 27, 28, 29, 32, 34, 48, 74, 77, 85, 89-91
Arthur 13, 27
Attila 15, 39, 45-47

Bacaudae 18, 50, 52
Bases (for wargames figures) 35-37, 74
Boardgames 18
Bucellarii 8
Burgundians 12, 16, 19, 39, 45, 47

Campaigns 18, 68-72
Catafractarii 32, 35
Cataphracts 32, 35, 89
Chalons, Battle of 15, 45-47
Chnodommar 43
Clibanarii 32, 33, 35
Combat 84-86
Comitatus (Comitati) 8, 24, 25, 29, 32, 38, 74, 89, 90, 91
Command and control 74, 81-82
Committee games 18, 63-68

Dice 49, 78
Disguised scenario 43-45, 63, 65-68
Disorder 78

Experience 89

Federates (Foederati) 10, 11
Field Army 9, 10, 19, 21, 35, 48, 50, 66
Formations 78-79
Francisca 26
Franks 10, 12, 16, 24, 39, 40, 45-47, 71
Fritigern 43

Gallo-Romans 19,24
Gepids 19, 24, 40, 45-47
Goths 8, 11, 12, 19, 39, 57, 64

Huns 11, 15, 19, 27, 39, 45-47, 70, 71

Julian 10, 42, 43, 63, 65

Laager 43, 46
Limitanei 21, 22, 23
Lombards 19, 24

Missile fire 82-85
Moors 24, 88
Morale 73, 74, 75, 86
Movement 79, 81

Notitia Dignitatum 34

Organization (for wargames) 35-40, 74-75
Ostrogoths 11, 15, 17, 19, 24, 40, 43-47

Palatini (Palatine troops) 9, 19, 21, 66
Personal combat 91
Primani Legion 41, 73
Procopius 24, 74, 92
Pursuit 85, 87

Role-playing 18, 47, 69
Romano-British 19, 69
Rout 86-87

Sarmatians 35, 64
Saxons 12, 24, 25, 56, 69
Scale 20, 35
Set piece battles 41-47
Skirmish games 47-49
Spangenhelm 29, 31, 34
Spatha 26, 29
Speeches 91
Stilicho 11, 27, 69
Stands (see bases)
Strasbourg, Battle of 7, 19, 21, 41-43, 45, 63, 73
Suebi (Swabians) 12, 16, 19, 41

Troop types 38-40, 75-78

Uniforms 29, 32, 34

Valens 43-45, 63,68
Vandals 8, 11, 12, 15, 19, 24, 71
Vegitius 32
Visigoths 11, 12, 14, 16, 18, 19, 24, 43-47, 69, 71

Warlords and Rebels (game scenario) 49-62

95